UNSOLVED MYSTERIES

UNSOLVED MYSTERIES

Text by Mandy Woods

An Hachette UK Company
www.hachette.co.uk

Summersdale Publishers Ltd
Part of Octopus Publishing Group Limited
Carmelite House
50 Victoria Embankment
LONDON
EC4Y 0DZ
UK

www.summersdale.com

Printed and bound by CPI Group (UK) Ltd, Croydon, CR0 4YY

ISBN: 978-1-80007-990-8

Substantial discounts on bulk quantities of Summersdale books are available to corporations, professional associations and other organizations. For details contact general enquiries: telephone: +44 (0) 1243 771107 or email: enquiries@summersdale.com.

UNSOLVED MYSTERIES

Unexplained Events and Paranormal Phenomena from Around the World

JAMIE KING

summersdale

DISCLAIMER

The author and the publishers make no claim that any of these stories have any basis in fact. They are merely mysteries that have enjoyed popularity in the public domain in some form or another. Such stories are reproduced herein for entertainment purposes only and are not intended to be taken literally.

CONTENTS

INTRODUCTION

Back in the 1970s, the American TV detective Lieutenant Columbo had a hallmark habit of returning one last time to the scene of an unsolved crime, where he would ask someone apparently uninvolved in the crime "just one more thing..." And then he'd ask an incisive critical question, the answer to which would invariably lead to him pointing the finger of guilt at that person, thereby solving the crime.

In the real world, however, some cases are simply unsolvable. But it's not just crimes that often go unsolved. People go missing for good after saying they're just popping out to the shop; ships sail off into the horizon and are never seen again; aircraft suddenly vanish off the radar mid-flight. There is almost always a great deal of speculation as to what happened. But often, that's all it is – fruitless conjecture, and, with no solid answers ever surfacing, they remain forever shrouded in mystery.

But that lack of resolution is what makes these cases all the more intriguing, because, as any true lover of mysteries will tell you, the as yet unsolved ones will not leave us alone. They dominate our thoughts as we puzzle over what could have happened; we want to explore all the angles. Once a mystery is neatly solved, it's no longer beguiling. Our curiosity is satisfied, and we move on. Unsolved mysteries spark the imagination and set us off down all sorts of tantalizing alleyways – both real and metaphorical – in a bid to reach the truth.

This book is divided into six chapters, each one dealing with a distinct category of unsolved mystery: strange disappearances, ghosts and haunted places, mystifying landmarks, suspicious deaths, legendary creatures, alien encounters and UFO sightings. There are stories from all over the world, and from hundreds – even thousands – of years ago right up to the present day.

Within these chapters, too, there are a few record-breakers: the first ransom kidnapping to be widely reported in America; the first death in pursuit of a UFO; the world's most documented UFO sighting; the world's oldest artworks; and "the missingest man in New York".

The accounts here are often just scratching the surface of the full stories, with articles and books devoted to searches for the truth.

A handful of the mysteries presented in the following pages were, in the end, solved – at least to a degree. But most weren't. Or haven't been yet. But, as you'll read, that didn't stop people from becoming obsessed with trying to find answers to these puzzling conundrums, sometimes devoting their entire lives to the quest.

Despite the fictional Columbo's uncanny ability to solve the most unsolvable crimes, in the real world of unsolved mysteries, it often turns out that no conclusion can ever be definitive. And that, as you're about to discover, is what makes these cases so compelling.

STRANGE
DISAPPEARANCES

A woman sets off on a 30-minute drive to watch her fiancé play softball but never gets there. She is never seen again. The leader of a colony of adventurous pioneers returns with new supplies to find they've completely vanished. All 115 of them. A world-famous murder-mystery writer creates her own mystery by disappearing for an 11-day hiatus that sets the world buzzing with concern, and more than a little intrigue. But she's never able – or willing – to explain what happened.

It's these stories, and more of their kind, that make up this chapter about strange disappearances. If a person says they're just nipping down the road to buy a pint of milk, we expect them to be back within the hour. When a day, then a week, then a year go by and they haven't returned, lives are flipped upside down. Those left wondering what happened to their loved one may spend the rest of their lives trying to fathom the unfathomable.

Whether it's people, ships or planes that appear to have vanished off the face of the Earth, their stories make compelling reading...

THE LOST COLO NY OF ROANOKE

In the summer of 1587, a group of about 115 English settlers arrived on Roanoke Island, off the coast of what is now the US state of North Carolina, intending to form the first permanent English outpost in the New World. It was Sir Walter Raleigh's project for Queen Elizabeth I; a group had established a claim on the same island two years earlier but left after problems with supplies and the local native population.

Later in 1587, the governor of the new colony, John White, sailed back to England to gather more supplies, leaving his wife and daughter on the island, together with his baby granddaughter, Virginia Dare, the first English child to be born in the Americas. He arrived back on English shores just as the 150 ships of the Spanish Armada were sighted – according to legend, by Sir Francis Drake during a game of bowls on Plymouth Hoe – signalling King Philip II's planned invasion of England. As a result, White's ship was one of the many called on by Queen Elizabeth I to confront the powerful fleet.

By the end of 1588, the English had proved victorious over the Spanish ships, the few that remained intact having limped home in October, and White was now free to continue to amass supplies for the Roanoke colony. He returned there in August 1590, having been away for three long years.

But on his arrival, despite sighting occasional elusive plumes of smoke, he found no trace of the colony or its people, and nothing to tell him what had happened apart from the word "Croatoan" (the name of a neighbouring island inhabited by a Native American tribe of the same name) carved into a wooden post, and "Cro" carved into a tree. The houses and boats had gone. There was no indication of any struggle, but he would never see any of the colonists – including his family – again. He tried reaching Croatoan but was forced, by rough seas and a lost anchor, to abandon the mission.

Walter Raleigh rather opportunistically concluded that the colonists had merely relocated, which meant his claim on the land was still valid.

There were numerous attempts over the subsequent centuries to discover what became of the "lost colony" of Roanoke, still debated today. Perhaps the most obvious scenario, given the clue on the wooden post, is that the people were killed or abducted by the neighbours of Croatoan (now Hatteras Island). Others think they might have attempted to sail back to England themselves somehow and got lost at sea. Still others propose that they were butchered by the Spanish invaders who had travelled up the coast from Florida – or simply might have moved ashore and been absorbed into a friendly tribe.

The "Lost Colony Y DNA Project", which started in 2007, was aimed at trying to identify the ancestors of the lost Roanoke colonists through DNA testing, focusing on the paternal line. A call was put out by researchers for any individuals to come forward whose surname matched any of the colonists' surnames, whose family tree could be traced back to North

Carolina in the 1700s, who had a Native American ancestor originating from an eastern North Carolina tribe, or who had any oral history relating to the lost colony. The process was expected to be a slow one, but the hope remains that one day some further knowledge will come to light as to what became of the 115 lost colonists of Roanoke.

SS WARATAH: AUSTRALIA'S TITANIC?

On 26 July 1909, the steamship SS *Waratah* was on her second voyage from Australia to Europe. The 832-mile leg of the journey from Durban to Cape Town would take three days. She was carrying 211 passengers and 1,000 tons of cargo.

The area is famous for bad weather, and on those days, increasingly strong winds and rough seas developed into a hurricane. The captain of a ship the *Waratah* passed – its last confirmed sighting – said it was the worst weather he had ever experienced during his 13 years at sea. But the ship's hull had been built with eight watertight compartments which, an article in the *Albany Advertiser* reported at the time, supposedly rendered her "practically immune from any danger of sinking".

At least one person who had sailed on the *Waratah*, however, had his doubts about the ship's unsinkability. Claude G. Sawyer, an engineer and experienced sea traveller, had his passage booked through to Cape Town but decided to disembark at Durban, sending a cable to his wife saying, "Thought Waratah top-heavy, landed Durban".

Its failure to appear in Cape Town on the scheduled date of 29 July didn't initially cause alarm.

When the ship had still not appeared by 1 August, however, the first search effort got under way, but was forced to give up because of continuing bad weather. Those that followed were equally fruitless, despite one false sighting. It seemed the ship had vanished – without any trace. The ship was listed as officially missing months later, on 15 December 1909, though relatives of the passengers made one further unsuccessful attempt to locate the ship in 1910.

At the later inquiry in London into the ship's disappearance, Sawyer gave a further reason for his decision to leave the ship early – namely, a series of disturbing dreams he'd had on the voyage to Durban. He claimed to have seen a man "dressed in a very peculiar dress, which I had never seen before, with a long sword in his right hand, which he seemed to be holding between us. In the other hand he had a rag covered with blood." Sawyer took the dreams as a warning to leave the ship at the earliest opportunity – a decision that saved his life.

The *Waratah* was gone, but not forgotten. Decades later, Emlyn Brown, a South African former naval recruit, led a series of no less than 14 expeditions to find the wreckage, beginning in 1983. In 2004, having spent 22 years looking for the *Waratah*, Brown gave up the search, saying, "I've exhausted all the options. I now have no idea where to look."

His efforts are documented in his 2017 book *The Mystery Runs Deep*, which also claims to expose the true story of the ship's owner, the Blue Anchor Line (which went into liquidation the following year), and the decisions that may have led to the ship's demise. Despite claims of wreckage being spotted – pieces of cork and timber on the South African coast, a life jacket with the name *Waratah* washed up as far away as New

Zealand – strangely there has never been any confirmed trace of the ship or its occupants.

Is it true, as some believe, that a freak wave capsized the ship, its cargo shifting and affecting the ship's stability? Did a whirlpool suck it down? Or was it that one of its coal bunkers exploded? Just three years later, the similarly unsinkable *Titanic* would go down, with more than 1,500 lives lost, leading to the *Waratah* being referred to as the "*Titanic* of the southern seas" or "Australia's *Titanic*".

AGATHA CHRISTIE: MYSTERY WITHOUT A MURDER

The novelist Agatha Christie was 36 years old and at the height of her fame, already a world-renowned writer of murder mysteries. On 3 December 1926, she kissed her seven-year-old daughter Rosalind goodnight at 9.30 p.m., left her in the care of the maids with a note saying she was going for a drive, and pulled away from her Berkshire home in her Morris Cowley.

Her car was found abandoned next morning – apparently crashed and partially buried in the bushes at Newlands Corner, the headlights on and a suitcase and coat on the back seat. A nearby beauty spot, the Silent Pool, said to be haunted by a medieval woodcutter's daughter who drowned, was dredged but nothing untoward was found. One of the largest manhunts ever mounted got under way with more than 1,000 police, volunteers, bloodhounds and, for the first time ever, aeroplanes, put on the case.

Since the strange disappearance resembled one of Christie's own mystery plots, the crime writers Sir Arthur Conan Doyle and Dorothy L. Sayers, creators of the fictional detectives Sherlock Holmes and Lord Peter Wimsey respectively, were asked to use their specialist knowledge to help in the search.

Conan Doyle, who had an interest in the occult, took one of Christie's gloves to a famous medium, but no useful answers were forthcoming.

As the hunt continued, suspicion began to mount. Had her husband, Archie Christie, who was known to have had a string of mistresses, murdered her? Or was the incident nothing more than a publicity stunt aimed at promoting Christie's latest book, *The Murder of Roger Ackroyd*? News of her disappearance had spread around the world, making the front page of *The New York Times*.

It was 11 days after her disappearance, at the elegant Swan Hydro (now the Old Swan Hotel) in Harrogate in the north of England, 200 miles from Berkshire, that one of the hotel's orchestra musicians recognized a guest. Oddly, she had checked in under the surname of her husband's current mistress, Neale. The police were alerted, and Christie's husband immediately went to collect his wife.

But the mystery of why she had vanished and what had happened to her between 3 and 14 December was no closer to being solved, because Christie herself claimed to remember nothing. Her husband put it down to a total memory loss as a result of the car crash. However, the biographer Andrew Norman believed the author was in a suicidal frame of mind when she vanished, and was suffering from a psychogenic trance, sometimes brought on by depression. "Her state of mind was very low and she writes about it later through the character of Celia in her autobiographical novel *Unfinished Portrait*," he wrote.

Christie made a full recovery, but her 11-day hiatus did seem to provide the jolt she needed: just over a year later she divorced her unfaithful husband and married the archaeologist

Sir Max Mallowman. She went on to become the best-selling fiction writer of all time, her novels being outsold only by the Bible and Shakespeare.

But the mystery of what happened to Christie during those lost days remains one that even her own famous sleuth Miss Marple would probably not have been able to solve.

THE DINGO DID IT

In August 1980, young Queensland couple Lindy and Michael Chamberlain drove to Uluru, then more commonly known as Ayers Rock, in the remote Northern Territory of Australia, with their two young children and baby Azaria, just nine weeks old. They arrived late on 16 August, set up at the campground, and spent the next day exploring. While Michael was with the boys, Lindy visited a cave with Azaria in her arms, and saw a dingo – a wild dog native to Australia – staring up at them. It gave her an uneasy feeling.

That night, as they enjoyed a barbecue with other campers, a dingo was seen nearby and Michael threw it a crust of bread. Soon after, Lindy decided it was bedtime for Azaria and laid her down in the tent with her brother Aiden, but it was not long before she heard crying and went back to check on her. Lindy was suddenly heard to shout, "My God, my God, the dingo's got my baby!" There were blood and pawprints leading out of the tent.

Hundreds of people joined in a search, looking for the baby that the dingo had dragged out of the tent. Her body was never found.

International media interest in the story was intense, and for the first time ever in Australia, the findings of the inquest

19

were broadcast live on television. Allegations were made against the couple for their Seventh-Day Adventist religious beliefs, including false claims that the church was a cult that killed babies, that the name "Azaria" meant "Sacrifice in the Wilderness" (in fact it means "Helped by God"). The Jonestown incident had happened just two years earlier. It was noted that the couple didn't seem distraught enough, and that although Lindy had been carrying a bundle, nobody had actually seen the baby.

Amid accusations of newspaper and TV reports sensationalizing the tragedy, Lindy was tried for murder. Foetal haemoglobin was claimed to have been found in the Chamberlains' car and was presented as a key piece of evidence, despite it being very similar to adult blood. Although nobody could really say for sure what happened that night at the campground, on 29 October 1982, Lindy was convicted of the murder of her daughter Azaria and sentenced to life in prison. Michael was convicted of being an accessory and given a suspended sentence.

After all legal options for appealing their convictions had been exhausted, the Chamberlains' fate looked sealed. Until, that is, in 1986, a British tourist by the name of David Brett went for an ill-advised evening climb up the slopes of Uluru, missing his footing and falling to his death. Owing to the vast size of the rock and the difficult nature of the surrounding terrain, it was eight days before his remains were retrieved from beneath the bluff where he had tripped – an area full of dingo lairs. When police went down there to search for the dead climber's bones (by now scattered), they discovered Azaria's matinee jacket, which had been missing ever since the baby disappeared almost six years previously.

Lindy was immediately released from prison and the case reopened. On 15 September 1988, all the convictions against the Chamberlains were unanimously overturned and the couple were exonerated. Two years later they were awarded a sum of money for wrongful imprisonment that covered less than a third of their legal expenses.

It wasn't until 2012, at a fourth inquest into Azaria Chamberlain's disappearance, that a coroner finally ruled that a dingo had been responsible for the baby girl's death. Over the course of the previous three decades, most of the evidence that had originally been used to convict Lindy was later rejected. The disturbing case is now used to show how media portrayal and biased opinion – attempting to solve a mystery too easily – can adversely affect the outcome of a trial.

GLENN MILLER'S LAST-MINUTE HITCH

On 15 December 1944, a small single-engine aircraft bound for Paris took off from an airfield in Bedford, England, with a pilot and two passengers – one of them the legendary American big-band leader Glenn Miller. It was just months before the end of the Second World War, and Miller was serving in England as a US Army officer, providing band music and radio shows for the American troops in Europe.

By then, 40-year-old Miller, also famous as a composer, arranger, trombone player and recording artist, had a string of hit tunes with his orchestra, including "Moonlight Serenade", "Chattanooga Choo Choo" and "In the Mood". He had been ordered to fly to Paris ahead of his orchestra's relocation there in time for Christmas, but bad weather conditions had led to two previous flights being cancelled. Growing increasingly impatient with the delay, on the third day, without telling anyone, Miller hitched a ride with an acquaintance, Lieutenant Colonel Norman Baessell. However, the plane never reached Paris.

When Baessell's UC-64A Norseman went missing, three days passed before the army realized that Miller had been on board. Another five days went by before Miller's wife was notified of her husband's disappearance, and it wasn't until the following day – Christmas Eve – that a press release was finally issued.

Despite extensive search operations, no trace of the plane or its occupants was found, and on 20 January 1945, a UK Board of Inquiry determined that the aircraft had gone down over the English Channel due to a combination of human error, mechanical failure and bad weather conditions. A year and a day after the plane went missing, all three occupants were officially declared dead, even though their bodies had never been recovered.

The mystery of the case led to countless sensationalist conspiracy theories springing up over the years. Among these, there was speculation that Miller had been a spy; that he had never boarded the plane but was instead assassinated while on a secret mission for General Eisenhower; that his plane was brought down by friendly fire; that he had faked his death and fled to South America; or that he had come to a sordid end in a Parisian brothel…

Although it is unlikely ever to be proved conclusively, the plane most probably went down over a treacherously icy English Channel when its fuel lines froze. The pilot, 20-year-old John Morgan, would have been flying very low because of heavy cloud cover, so when the engine cut out, he would have only had about eight seconds to react before it plunged into the water, disintegrating on impact and killing those on board instantly.

In 2019, 75 years after Miller disappeared, a fisherman claimed that in 1987, when he was fishing off the coast of Dorset, his nets had snagged the remains of an aircraft but he had let it fall back to the seabed. Later, seeing photos of the UC-64A Norseman carrying Miller, he thought it looked the same. Although the location was further west than the areas previously searched, it remains a possibility that it was indeed the plane carrying Miller.

Miller's age, his marital status and his poor eyesight would have been more than sufficient grounds for him to have legitimately avoided being called up to serve during the war. Yet, despite being at the height of his career and earning $20,000 a week from his musical activities, he was utterly determined to play his part in the war effort. Rejected by the US Navy, he ended up doing his military duty in the army instead. His dogged determination ultimately led to his demise, and to one of the most enduring unsolved mysteries of modern times.

THE TOWER OF DOOM

More than five centuries have passed since two boys went missing, aged 12 and nine, in mysterious circumstances. Depicted as wearing black, with long fair hair, they are widely believed to have been murdered by their uncle – but it remains one of history's most enduring and fascinating cold cases. What became of the Princes in the Tower?

The princes were the 12-year-old Edward, destined to be King Edward V of England, and his younger brother, Richard of Shrewsbury, Duke of York. They had grown up in a time of civil war, the War of the Roses, with rival Plantagenets fighting for the crown. Their father, King Edward IV, died prematurely on 9 April 1483 after a short illness during which he appointed his brother, Richard, Duke of Gloucester, as Lord Protector, to look after the new young king.

Gloucester was said to have publicly pledged his loyalty to Edward V, yet by the end of April he had taken complete control of the boy, whom he lodged in the Tower of London on 19 May. Although it was the traditional residence of new monarchs prior to their coronation, on 16 June, the younger brother was also brought to the tower, and the date of the coronation postponed indefinitely.

On 22 June 1483, in a sermon at the open-air pulpit of St Paul's Cross by Canon Ralph Shaw, brother of the Lord Mayor of London, Gloucester was declared the House of York's only legitimate heir to the throne. A subsequent Act of Parliament declared his brother's marriage to the widow Elizabeth Woodville invalid and their offspring illegitimate. Within a couple of weeks, Gloucester was crowned King Richard III of England, at which point the boys were taken into the inner recesses of the Tower. There were no further recorded sightings of them.

Although there is no direct evidence that the princes were murdered, many believe that Richard was responsible for their deaths. Writing a few decades later, Sir Thomas More in his *History of King Richard III* pointed the finger at Richard's servant Sir James Tyrrell, saying he had hired killers. In his 1593 play *King Richard III*, William Shakespeare echoed this. Other suspects include Henry Stafford, 2nd Duke of Buckingham, and King Henry VII – though he was out of the country.

Then in 1674, when workmen in the Tower of London unearthed a wooden box containing two small human skeletons, it seemed likely that a 200-year-old mystery had finally been solved. The remains weren't the first children's skeletons to be found in the Tower, but their location partially matched that given by Sir Thomas More. Some velvet was also said to have been found with them – a fabric closely associated with royalty. King Charles II had them placed in an urn and interred in Westminster Abbey, with a monument designed by Sir Christopher Wren and inscribed with the story of their discovery.

In 1933, the remains were removed for more scientific examination, and experts concluded that they did indeed belong to two children of around the same ages as the unfortunate princes. But strangely, there was no attempt to determine the sex of the skeletons or how they died.

STRANGE DISAPPEARANCES

There's just one more thing... In 1789, workmen had accidentally broken into the vault of Edward IV and Elizabeth Woodville at Windsor Castle and discovered an adjoining vault containing the coffins of two unidentified children. It was assumed at the time that these were two other children of the royal couple – George, Duke of Bedford and Mary of York – but in fact their coffins were subsequently found elsewhere. No further attempt was made to identify the remains discovered in 1789, but perhaps the investigation is not yet over and the questions that still remain will one day be answered.

WHO GOT HOFFA?

When the American labour union organizer Jimmy Hoffa vanished at the age of 62 on 30 July 1975, it may not have come as a complete surprise.

Hoffa had been a union activist from an early age, and from 1957 he was president of the truck drivers' union, the International Brotherhood of Teamsters, which, under his leadership, became the largest union by membership in the US. During this time, however, Hoffa became involved with organized crime and the Mafia, which exerted great influence in trucking unions throughout that era.

His friendships with gangsters would lead to him facing criminal charges and prison terms throughout the 1960s. As US attorney general, Robert Kennedy had a "Get Hoffa" squad of law-enforcement officials working on convicting Hoffa of Mob-related charges, and in 1967, Hoffa was jailed for 13 years for bribery and fraud.

Although initially trying to continue to act as union leader from his prison cell, by 1971, still in prison, he resigned as the Teamsters president. Later that year, his prison sentence, which still had eight years to run, was commuted by US president, Richard Nixon, though he was not permitted to have any further union involvement until 1980. Despite this condition, and although he had lost a lot of support in the major union region of Detroit, by 1973 Hoffa was planning to seize the leadership again.

One Mafia boss who was particularly opposed to this was Anthony Provenzano, a one-time friend of Hoffa who had become an enemy following a feud while both were serving time in Pennsylvania. When Hoffa asked him to support his leadership bid, Provenzano is reported to have refused and threatened to pull Hoffa's guts out and kidnap his grandchildren. At least two of Provenzano's union opponents are known to have been murdered, and others who spoke out against him were assaulted.

Two other Mafia figures, the Giacalone brothers, Anthony and Vito, offered to mediate between the two men, and they set up a "peace meeting" at the Machus Red Fox restaurant in a Detroit suburb at 2 p.m. on 30 July 1975. At around 2.30 p.m., Hoffa called his wife from a payphone close to the restaurant to complain that he had been stood up by the men. A few minutes before 3 p.m., he is thought to have left the location without a struggle, and was seen by one witness in the back of a maroon "Lincoln or Mercury" car with three other people.

Hoffa was never seen again. Despite his son filing a missing-person report the following evening and a $200,000 reward being offered by his family for any information about his disappearance, after years of investigation no definitive conclusion was ever reached as to what became of him. Anthony Giacalone and Provenzano both had an alibi for that afternoon, and, indeed, denied ever having scheduled a meeting there with Hoffa. Hoffa's family suspected that his foster son, Charles O'Brien, may have had something to do with his disappearance, having borrowed a maroon Mercury car owned by Joe Giacalone, Anthony's son, earlier that day, ostensibly to deliver fish.

In 2020, one Frank Cappola, who was a teenager at the time of Hoffa's disappearance, claimed before he died that he knew what had happened to Hoffa's body. But a search of a New Jersey landfill site, where it was claimed Hoffa had been buried in a steel drum, yielded nothing. We still don't know for sure who got Hoffa, or how they did it.

#WHEREISPENGSHUAI

On 2 November 2021, in a lengthy post on the Chinese social media platform Weibo, 35-year-old professional tennis player Peng Shuai accused a top Chinese politician of sexually assaulting her three years previously. Within minutes, the post – the most significant accusation of China's #MeToo movement – had been removed, anyone forwarding a screenshot of it was blocked, and the name "Peng Shuai" was no longer searchable on the Chinese internet. For a while, even the word "tennis" was blocked, as was the name of China's former vice-premier, 75-year-old Zhang Gaoli, the man whom Peng had accused. And Peng herself vanished from the public eye.

It was revealed that Peng had consensual sex a decade earlier with the politician, then after a long period of no contact, Zhang invited her to play tennis with him and his wife, subsequently forcing her to have sex with him in his house. In her post, Peng wrote, "You were always afraid I would make recordings and keep them as evidence. In fact I have no evidence or proof other than my own word. But even if it's just me, like an egg hitting a rock, or a moth to the flame, courting self-destruction, I'll tell the truth about you."

When Peng had not resurfaced after ten days, the hashtag #WhereIsPengShuai appeared on Twitter and was rapidly picked up by the international tennis community, many of whom – including Serena Williams, Billie Jean King and Rafael Nadal – denounced the censorship of Peng and expressed concerns for her safety. On 14 November, Steve Simon, head of the Women's Tennis Association (WTA), called for the Chinese authorities to investigate Peng's allegations and to stop censoring her.

On 17 November, the Chinese Communist Party's publicity department tweeted a message it claimed was from Peng to Simon, written in English and declaring that her allegations of sexual assault had not been true. She also claimed that she was simply "resting at home and everything is fine". The message ended, "Thank you again for caring about me."

Simon said the suspicious tweet only increased his concern for her safety, adding that he had tried to communicate with her by various means, "to no avail". Within days, equally suspicious photos and videos were posted by China's state television organization showing Peng, among other things, eating at a Beijing restaurant with her coach. Although Peng didn't speak in the video, the coach, as if to date-stamp it, says to her, "It's November 21 tomorrow, right?" A Chinese civil-rights lawyer pointed out that the posts only showed that Peng was alive, not that she was free.

On 3 December, the WTA suspended all tournaments in China and Hong Kong. Sixteen days later, a Singaporean newspaper published a video interview with Peng in which she once again denied that she had ever claimed to have been sexually assaulted. She also said that she was not under house arrest or being monitored, and that she had only stopped travelling and competing because of the Covid-19 pandemic, which was sweeping the world at the time.

Once again, the video only increased concern for her safety, as did subsequent attempts by the Chinese authorities to convince the world that she was OK.

When officials at the 2022 Australian Open tennis tournament initially banned fans from wearing T-shirts bearing the slogan "Where is Peng Shuai", retired tennis player Martina Navratilova tweeted: "That's just pathetic. The @wta stands pretty much alone on this!!! #whereisPengShuai." It's a question whose true answer would remain worryingly unknown and until the WTA meets Peng, tournaments will not resume in China.

RICHEY EDWARDS: OVER THE BRIDGE AND FAR AWAY

Just over two weeks after a troubled musician vanished, leaving in his wake a number of enigmatic clues, his car was found abandoned close to a known suicide spot. But even though the Welsh rock star Richey Edwards was declared to be legally "presumed dead" 13 years later, reported sightings around the world and the fact that no body was ever found left an abiding air of mystery around his disappearance at the age of 27 on 1 February 1995.

In 2019, with the cooperation of his sister Rachel, the book *Withdrawn Traces: Searching for the Truth about Richey Manic* suggested that he had staged the disappearance and was living on a kibbutz in Israel, and in 2020 the charity Missing People put out an appeal for information about him.

The writer of dark, political, intellectual lyrics, Edwards was famous as the main songwriter and rhythm guitarist of the Welsh rock band Manic Street Preachers, becoming its fourth member in 1989 after being the band's driver and roadie. He spoke openly about his severe depression, anorexia and self-harming, carving the words "4 Real" into his forearm with a razor blade in 1991 after being questioned by a journalist as to how serious he was about his art. The wound required 18 stitches.

In a concert at the London Astoria just before Christmas 1994, Edwards ended the set by smashing his guitar, the rest of the band following suit. A month later, on 23 January 1995, he gave an interview to the Japanese magazine *Music Life*. In the fortnight before his disappearance, he withdrew £200 a day from a bank machine.

Edwards disappeared on the day he was due to fly to the US on a promotional tour. The previous night, he gave a friend the book *Novel with Cocaine*, telling her to read the introduction, describing how the Russian author stayed in a mental asylum before vanishing. He also gave his on/off girlfriend, with whom he had recently broken up, a gift-wrapped box containing books, videos and a note saying, "I love you".

Seventeen days passed between Edwards' disappearance and his car being found abandoned near the Severn Bridge. For some of that time he is thought to have lived in the car. He is known to have crossed the bridge in the early hours of the morning, but although it is widely believed that Edwards jumped from the bridge, some who knew him are not so sure. The year before, Edwards himself said of suicide: "In terms of the 'S' word, that does not enter my mind. And it never has done, in terms of an attempt. Because I am stronger than that. I might be a weak person, but I can take pain." And since 1995, there have been reported sightings of him in a market in Goa, India and in the Canary Islands, among other places.

Fourteen years after Edwards disappeared, and a year after he was officially presumed dead on 28 November 2008, his band released the album *Journal for Plague Lovers*, consisting entirely of lyrics he had left behind. But for some, to this day, hope continues to linger that, as Paul Rees, editor of the former music magazine *Q*, said, "he might just walk through the door".

MARY CELESTE: ABANDON SHIP

When the American merchant ship *Mary Celeste* set sail from New York City on 7 November 1872, bound for the Italian port of Genoa, nothing seemed amiss. There were ten people on board, including Captain Briggs, his wife and their two-year-old daughter, as well as a cargo of more than 1,700 barrels of alcohol. Yet somewhere along the way everyone on board vanished, never to be seen again, alive or dead.

It was ten days after the last log entry, dated 25 November, that the vessel was spotted by the British brig *Dei Gratia* moving erratically somewhere off the Azores Islands. When the crew boarded the *Mary Celeste*, they discovered that it was completely deserted, with nothing to indicate what had happened, though the vessel appeared to have been abandoned in a hurry. Although the ship was still seaworthy, the hold was under 3 feet of water, all the lifeboats had gone and the contents of the main cabin had been somewhat disturbed – though the cargo of alcohol remained intact.

According to the court record from the salvage hearings that were later conducted, "[t]he Galley was in a bad state, the stove was knocked out of its place, and the cooking utensils were strewn around. The whole ship was a thoroughly wet mess. The Captain's bed was not fit to sleep in and had to be dried."

The crew of the *Dei Gratia* sailed the abandoned vessel to Gibraltar, where Attorney General Frederick Solly-Flood was put in charge of the salvage hearings. Although he suspected foul play – mutiny by the crew of the *Mary Celeste*, piracy by the crew of the *Dei Gratia* or another vessel given the nature of the cargo, or conspiracy to carry out insurance or salvage fraud, since the captains of the two ships were said to be acquainted – there was no convincing evidence to support any of these explanations. A salvage award was therefore made – though with suspicions not having entirely been laid to rest, it was a relatively low payout of one sixth of the insured value.

The *Mary Celeste* then sailed on to Genoa to deliver its cargo without further incident. That, however, did not stop the mysterious story of the deserted ship from morphing into legendary status, aided by Sir Arthur Conan Doyle's 1884 short story *J. Habakuk Jephson's Statement*, which takes the form of a first-person testimony by a survivor of a deserted ship. Although based on the *Mary Celeste*, in this story the ship became the *Marie Celeste* – a name that has become synonymous with finding a normally busy place inexplicably deserted.

Filling the void created by the somewhat inconclusive findings of the salvage hearings, more outlandish theories have been put forward, blaming the intoxicating effects on the crew of the alcoholic fumes floating up from the stored cargo, implicating a giant-squid attack, or putting it all down to paranormal intervention.

It's agreed that something serious must have happened for the captain and crew to have abandoned a sound ship still carrying plenty of provisions. The fact that the sounding rod, the tool for assessing water in the hold, was found on deck may suggest that Briggs believed they were about to sink. An erroneous reading and a faulty pump could have caused them to take to the lifeboat. Others have cited natural phenomena, such as a submarine earthquake or a waterspout, as possible explanations for the otherwise unaccountable, and certainly haunting desertion of the *Mary Celeste*.

AMELIA EARHART: NO SIGN ATOLL

By 1937, American pilot Amelia Earhart had set a number of aviation records, including, in 1932, becoming the first woman to fly solo across the Atlantic Ocean. Born in Kansas, she appears in photographs with cropped hair and a smile; she promoted commercial air travel, wrote books and formed an organization of women pilots.

Earhart was 39 years old and making her second attempt to fly around the world when she and her navigator, Fred Noonan, took off from Lae, New Guinea on 2 July, bound for Howland Island, a tiny uninhabited coral atoll in the Pacific Ocean. They were close to completing their 29,000-mile journey back to Oakland, California, where they had set out from on 21 May. But they lost contact with the *Itasca*, the US Coast Guard cutter that was awaiting their arrival, and never made it to Howland.

It's possible that, despite the aviators' experience, the small aircraft encountered difficulties due to overcast skies, ran out of fuel and crashed, to be lost in the ocean. That was the US Navy's official conclusion.

According to another theory, however, when the pair couldn't find Howland Island – even though in her last radio transmission Earhart had reported being on the correct coordinates – they continued for another 350 nautical miles, making an emergency landing on Nikumaroro (then called Gardner Island) and survived there as castaways for as long as their supplies lasted. When navy aircraft flew over the atoll a week after Earhart disappeared, although finding no trace of the aviators or their plane, they did report seeing signs of recent habitation, even though it had been uninhabited since 1892. If the plane had been set down on the reef around the island, it could have floated off and sunk.

Earhart was declared legally dead in January 1939 but in 1940, remains of a human skeleton were found on Nikumaroro. The bones were measured by a physician, who concluded that they came from a man. Strangely, the bones were later lost, but in 2018, in cooperation with the International Group for Historic Aircraft Recovery (TIGHAR), the University of Tennessee analyzed the measurements and decided that the bones were, in fact, most likely from a female and that they "have more similarity to Earhart than to 99 percent of individuals in a large reference sample".

An alternative theory claimed that Earhart and Noonan were captured by Japanese soldiers after being forced to land on the Marshall Islands, at the time controlled by Japan. From there they were taken to the Japanese island of Saipan, where they were tortured as US spies and later died – possibly by execution. This account was fuelled by stories being passed down the generations by contemporary Marshall Islanders of an "American lady pilot" who was held in custody on Saipan in 1937.

Some go even further and claim that Earhart and Noonan were in fact US spies and that their alleged circumnavigation was a cover-up for their espionage activities. However, in 1937, more than four years before the attack on Pearl Harbor, Japan was not an enemy of the US, making this aspect of the Japanese capture theory unlikely.

Others claimed that Earhart didn't die in Saipan but was repatriated, living under the assumed name of Irene Bolam, a New Jersey woman who vigorously denied the claims, despite having a pilot's licence and admitting to having known Earhart. But until wreckage is found of her twin-engine Lockheed Electra aircraft, speculation about what became of Earhart is likely to persist.

"YOU KNOW WHO I AM"

For 30 years, the Sicilian Mafia's "boss of all bosses", described by one Italian journalist as "the last godfather of the most ferocious generation of Mafiosi", effectively disappeared, evading capture.

With a reputation as a ruthless playboy with a taste for luxury, he used to chillingly boast that he could fill a cemetery with his victims – who included the pregnant girlfriend of a rival Mafia boss – and was on the "Most Wanted" list from 1993 after the Mafia orchestrated a string of bomb attacks. Accused of extortion, illegal waste dumping, money laundering and drug trafficking, in 2002 the head of the Cosa Nostra, Matteo Messina Denaro, was convicted of a string of murders – but couldn't be found.

The police didn't even know for sure what Italy's most wanted mobster looked like, with only an identikit image and short snippets of voice recordings to go by. The mysterious mobster had allegedly been spotted everywhere from the Netherlands to Venezuela but had proved completely elusive because of the smokescreen formed around him by the Mafia.

According to the Italian journalist Andrea Purgatori, "he was protected by a very dense network of complicities, deeply rooted and extremely powerful in Sicily and beyond". Despite the police wiretapping the homes of his relatives, arresting anyone suspected of protecting or helping him, and seizing business worth over £130 million, the 60-year-old Messina Denaro, whose assets were estimated at €4 billion, remained a free man.

Knowing from his family's bugged phone conversations that he was suffering from cancer, however, detectives gathered details of all male cancer patients the same age as Messina Denaro and born in the same part of western Sicily as him, Trapani. After narrowing down the list, the name that leaped out at them was Andrea Bonafede, the nephew of deceased Mafia boss Leonardo Bonafede. In January 2023, he had supposedly checked in at a private cancer clinic in Palermo, the Sicilian capital, but police knew that the real Andrea Bonafede had been nowhere near the city.

When a chemotherapy session was booked at the clinic under his name, more than 100 armed police and soldiers surrounded the premises. For a criminal who had dodged capture for three decades, his eventual arrest was remarkably straightforward, as if he was ready to be found. On being arrested, he put up no fight.

He was said to be "polite and soft-spoken". When a policeman asked him who he was, he replied, "You know who I am. I am Matteo Messina Denaro."

SHERGAR: GONE AT GUNPOINT

When the most famous and most valuable racehorse in the world was kidnapped and held to ransom, the world looked on with bated breath, willing the safe return of the beloved stallion. But he was never found, and more than 40 years later, the mystery of how gentle champion Shergar disappeared remains unsolved.

It was at 8 p.m. on 8 February 1983, during the height of the Northern Ireland conflict, that five-year-old Shergar and head groom Jim Fitzgerald were taken at gunpoint from the Ballymany Stud in County Kildare, Ireland, by a gang wearing balaclavas and wielding machine guns. They dumped Fitzgerald by the side of the road a few hours later, telling him the ransom for Shergar was £2 million. Although the father of six was able to find a phone box to call his brother, this was followed by calls to shareholders, the vet and others, and the police weren't contacted for eight hours, by which time it was impossible to track the kidnappers and Shergar. It was the day before a big racehorse sale, with lots of horseboxes on the road.

Shergar, worth over $15 million, was an obvious target, as one of his owners was the Aga Khan, not only spiritual leader to Shia Ismaili Muslims, but at the time one of the richest men in the world. However, after his first winning season, the stallion had been syndicated between 34 shareholders, all of whom would have had to agree to paying the fee that was being demanded.

The kidnappers quickly contacted the Aga Khan by telephone, carefully hanging up before the calls could be traced. They then agreed to negotiations with representatives of the syndicate, but a collective decision had been made not to pay the ransom, as that would have put every valuable racehorse in the world – many of whom were stabled in Ireland – in danger of being the next target. Even so, the Dublin police offered a large financial reward for the horse's safe return.

Four days after the kidnapping, photographs showing Shergar's head next to a copy of the *Irish Times*, purporting to show that he was still alive, were found at the Rosnaree Hotel in Drogheda. The syndicate told the gang more proof was needed.

The last phone call said, "The horse has had an accident. He's dead." No one would ever hear from Shergar's kidnappers again. By November the reward had increased substantially, thought to have been bolstered by shareholders who were uninsured for their loss, but it yielded no useful leads.

Many believe the gang were members of the Irish Republican Army, though the IRA never claimed responsibility. A former IRA member went on record as saying that Shergar was machine-gunned to death in a remote stable, and described the killing in gory detail. Shergar's body was never found, though he is thought to have either been buried in a bog in County Leitrim or dumped in the sea along the south coast.

The incident came just months after seven military horses had been among the victims of an IRA bomb attack in central

STRANGE DISAPPEARANCES

London, and the public grief and outrage was still palpable. The beloved racehorse's disappearance, and his probable violent end, created a worldwide media frenzy and a yearning to know what had become of him. The distinctive white blaze mark on his face, his four white "socks", and his endearing habit of running with his tongue hanging out had made him popular the world over, and decades later, his sad demise remained fresh in the memories of those who had lived through those gruelling four days in the winter of 1983.

MR KIDNAPPER

British estate agent Suzy Lamplugh, aged 25, went missing after meeting a client called "Mr Kipper" for a lunchtime house viewing at 37 Shorrolds Road in Fulham, London, on 28 July 1986. By 3.30 p.m., her colleagues were concerned she had not returned to the office and went to look for her. At 5.30 p.m., they called the police.

Her white Ford Fiesta was later found about a mile and a half away with doors unlocked, handbrake off and her purse inside.

Several witnesses reported seeing Lamplugh that afternoon. One of the most disturbing of these accounts was of a woman who matched the description of Lamplugh struggling with a man inside a black BMW parked opposite the house being viewed. She was beeping the horn in an apparent attempt to attract attention. In the witness's words, "She looked as though she was laughing, or she could have been screaming."

Her boyfriend and a male flatmate were questioned, but both had confirmed alibis. Confusing the issue was the fact that a mystery man had delivered red roses to her office days before. Sadly, although the young woman was never found, many believe it's clear what happened to her. John Cannan, a convicted rapist who was on day release from Wormwood Scrubs prison nearby, was considered a chief suspect. The following year, Cannan received three life sentences for the abduction and murder of Bristol businesswoman Shirley Banks.

Although he denied any link to Lamplugh's case, Cannan is known to have played games with the police. He used false number plates that included the letters SLP and when asked by detectives if he understood the significance of the number plate, he immediately replied that it could be seen as a reference to Lamplugh. If he enjoyed word games, perhaps it's significant that "Kipper" is kidnapper without the DNA. He also said on another occasion that he knew who killed Lamplugh and that this person was the same person responsible for the murder of Banks – for which he himself was serving three life sentences.

DNA evidence has been found that Lamplugh had been in a car owned by Cannan. Cannan was also known to have appeared at a house that was for sale in Shorrolds Road in the days before Lamplugh's disappearance. A young woman was alone in the house at the time, and claimed he acted strangely, but left as soon as her husband came home. In 2002, despite the Crown Prosecution Service deciding there was insufficient evidence to charge Cannan with Lamplugh's murder, the police, in an unusual move, stated that they believed he murdered her.

The Suzy Lamplugh Trust was set up in December 1986 by Lamplugh's parents, Paul and Diana Lamplugh, to raise awareness of personal safety and offer counselling and support to the relatives and friends of missing people. Both went to their graves not knowing what had become of their daughter.

BERMUDA TRIANGLE: FLOWN TO MARS

On 5 December 1945, Flight 19, comprising five US Navy torpedo-bombers with 14 men on board, took off from Fort Lauderdale, Florida for what should have been a routine three-hour training mission over the coast. Strangely, as they made their way back to base, the navigational and communication equipment on all five planes malfunctioned. In his last distorted message, the squadron leader instructed his men to prepare to ditch their aircraft because they had run out of fuel.

An hour later, having determined roughly where the downed planes of Flight 19 must be, a search-and-rescue Mariner aircraft took off to bring the 14 men back to safety. Twenty-three minutes after that, a tanker cruising off the Florida coast reported seeing an explosion. Despite a massive air and sea search being launched, neither the Mariner nor any of Flight 19's five planes was ever seen again – not even any debris or bodies. Although the US Navy maintained that storms must have destroyed the evidence, according to its official report, it was "as if they had flown to Mars". Why were no traces found of Flight 19 or the search-and-rescue aircraft?

STRANGE DISAPPEARANCES

The story appeared to confirm a growing suspicion – due to unexplained events dating back over 100 years – that there was a lethal area of ocean off the south-eastern tip of Florida where ships and aircraft simply disappeared. It wasn't until 1964 that the term "Bermuda Triangle" was coined by the author Vincent Gaddis in a magazine article. And once it had been coined, the term stuck.

More than 50 ships and 20 aircraft are claimed to have mysteriously vanished in the large area of sea roughly stretching from Florida to Puerto Rico to Bermuda, giving rise to countless theories ranging from the paranormal to the scientific. Although there is probably more than one explanation for the myriad disappearances, some of the theories are more plausible than others.

Some blame the agonic line – that is, the line around the Earth where no adjustment is needed for a compass needle to indicate true north. Failure to take this imaginary but crucial line into account when approaching the Bermuda Triangle could lead to significant navigational error and potential disaster. Alternatively, the massive rogue waves the area is known for may be responsible for sinking the missing vessels. If not magnetic anomalies or waves, then perhaps waterspouts, massive eruptions of methane gas from the seabed, or the strong pull of the Gulf Stream are to blame.

Or does it even exist at all? Lloyd's of London, the leading maritime insurance company, doesn't rate the Bermuda Triangle as any more dangerous than anywhere else. And according to the US Coast Guard, "[i]n a review of many aircraft and vessel losses in the area over the years, there has been nothing discovered that would indicate that casualties were the result of anything other than physical causes. No extraordinary factors have ever been identified." Similarly, a highly sceptical 1976 TV programme called *The Case of the Bermuda Triangle* declared, "When we've gone back to the original sources or the people involved, the mystery evaporates…"

In other words, disappointing as it may be to some, the Bermuda Triangle may simply be a figment of our collective imagination. On the other hand, depending on which paranormal writer you believe, the Bermuda Triangle could really be a result of UFOs, the lost continent of Atlantis, sea monsters, time/space warps or reverse gravity fields. And maybe the missing craft really are on Mars.

LITTLE BOY LOST

"Don't take candy from strangers!" Those familiar words of warning to children the world over are thought to have their origin in one of the first ransom kidnappings to receive widespread media coverage in America. It was one of the most disturbing, too, because to this day, the victim's fate remains unknown.

It was on 1 July 1874, while four-year-old Charley Ross and his five-year-old brother Walter were playing in front of their home in the well-heeled neighbourhood of Germantown in Philadelphia, Pennsylvania, that two men pulled up in a horse-drawn carriage and offered them candy and fireworks if they'd go for a ride with them. As the boys had seen the men offering candy in the preceding days, they accepted and were taken to a fireworks store, by which time Charley was crying and saying he wanted to go home. The men gave Walter 25 cents to go in and buy fireworks, but when he came out, the carriage was gone with Charley in it.

The boys' mother was away at the time, recovering from an illness. Two days later their father, dry-goods merchant Christian K. Ross, began receiving semi-literate ransom notes – 23 in total, mailed from post offices around the city, demanding $20,000 and threatening to kill Charley if he didn't cooperate.

The kidnappers assumed that Ross was wealthy, but due to the stock-market crash of the previous year, he was heavily in debt, with no choice but to go to the police.

The story quickly became national news. Millions of flyers were printed by the Pinkerton National Detective Agency, and attempts were made to meet the kidnappers and hand over the ransom money. Each time, they failed to appear, however, and eventually nothing more was heard from them.

Five months later, on 13 December 1874, two thieves broke into a judge's house in Brooklyn. During the burglary, both men were gunned down by an armed party the judge's brother had gathered to stop them. One of the thieves, William Mosher, was killed instantly. The other, Joe Douglas, made a confession as he lay dying.

"It's no use lying now," he is said to have told a witness. "Mosher and I stole Charley Ross." When asked where the boy was, Douglas replied, "Mosher knows. Ask him." On being told that Mosher was dead, he said, "Then God help his poor wife and family."

Charley's brother Walter was taken to New York City to see if he could identify Mosher and Douglas as the same men who had taken them for the carriage ride. Walter confirmed that they were. But now they were dead, and they alone had known where Charley was.

The boys' father published a book two years later and delivered lectures to raise money and keep the case in people's minds. The hunt for Charley continued all over the US, with hundreds of people falsely claiming to be the missing boy. One, a 69-year-old carpenter called Gustave Blair living in Arizona, claimed in 1934 that after the abduction he'd lived in a cave and had eventually been adopted by a man who told him he was

Charley Ross. Although Walter dismissed him as "a crank", his petition to be legally recognized as the real Charley Ross went uncontested. But the Ross family refused to recognize him and he was left out of any wills. In 2011, DNA analysis determined that Gustave Blair could not possibly have been Charley Ross.

Charley's parents never gave up looking for their son, spending around $60,000 on the quest, but 150 years on, the fate of the little boy remains unknown.

FOUL PLAY AT FOWLERVILLE

At around 7.30 p.m. on 24 May 1990, police officers were notified of a stationary vehicle sitting on the shoulder of Interstate 96 near Fowlerville, Michigan, with its engine still running and the lights and radio on. They merely had the car towed away, not viewing it as suspicious even though a woman's handbag, wallet and shoes and an open bottle of beer were still inside.

There was no damage to the car, either, which, it turned out, belonged to 30-year-old Paige Renkoski, last seen by passing motorists that afternoon on the shoulder of I-96 near Fowlerville talking to two African-American men who were standing next to a vehicle, perhaps a maroon-coloured minivan; another male may have been nearby. Some of the witnesses said she'd thrown her hands in the air, and one of the men had put his hand on her shoulder. She was never seen again, and her disappearance became one of Michigan's longest-running unsolved cases.

It was a motorist who had seen her talking to the men in the afternoon who alerted the police to the fact that her car was in the same place when he drove past again four hours later. Police sketches were produced of the men, based on witnesses' descriptions, and fingerprints were found, but no one was ever identified. It was not known why Renkoski had stopped to talk to them, although around that time, there had been a number of incidents of people flashing fake police badges at motorists to get them to stop. The motorist suggested she could have stopped if she'd seen someone she knew.

Earlier that day, blonde-haired, blue-eyed Renkoski, who worked as a substitute schoolteacher, had dropped her mother off at the local airport and then met a friend to have lunch in a park in Canton Township, where she went to a store and bought a beer. She was on her way to watch her fiancé's softball game, a 30-minute journey, when she pulled over on I-96. The friend and fiancé were eliminated from the inquiries, and with no other leads, the police, who didn't believe she had voluntarily gone missing, ruled the case a homicide even though her body was never found.

The case was reopened in 1999 when a Michigan State Police detective was delivered an anonymous tip by hand. It was a letter saying that Renkoski's remains were buried in a wooded area in Livingston County, with an accompanying map purporting to show exactly where. For reasons not generally known, the area wasn't excavated or forensically searched until 2011, when the case file was reviewed. Cadaver dogs indicated that there were human remains on a private property there, but nothing was found.

Renkoski's mother, Ardis, devoted the rest of her life to trying to find out what had happened to her daughter, and used the knowledge she had gained along the way to help other families in similar situations. Sadly, she died without knowing the answer, although her other daughter and her granddaughter continued her quest. When a person goes missing, our natural instinct is to keep hoping that one day, they may return.

HELP FIND BEN

It was a baking hot day in late July on the popular Greek island of Kos in the South Aegean, just a few miles from the shores of Turkey, and British toddler Ben was with his grandparents while his mother Kerry was working at a local hotel. The family had recently moved to Kos and the 21-month-old was playing outside the farmhouse that his grandparents, Eddie and Kristine Needham from Sheffield, were renovating.

It was around 2.30 p.m. on 24 July 1991 when the couple realized Ben was missing. At first, they thought he might have been taken for a ride by his uncle but when they couldn't find him, they alerted the police. Unfortunately, the police initially regarded them as suspects and in questioning them, delayed notifying the airport and port authorities about the missing child. As the days went by, there was still no sign of the boy.

After 11 days of intensive searching by police, army and fire brigade, the island's chief of police said, "We now believe we have searched every possible part of that area, and the boy is not there. It leaves us with a great mystery. We have no theories. We have no solutions." Ben's family were not prepared to give up so easily, however, and UK Prime Minister John Major intervened on their behalf.

Despite extensive police searches and questioning, however, Ben hasn't been seen since. Of more than 300 reported sightings of blond boys matching Ben's description, most occurred during 1991 and 1992, but further tests proved that none of them were the young English boy. In January 1993, the Greek Army resumed the search of the island, but to no avail. His family believed he had been kidnapped for adoption, or taken by child traffickers.

Several years later, the suggestion was put forward that Ben might have been accidentally buried in a pile of rubble that had been removed from the farmhouse by an excavator driver. In October 2012, British and Greek police began to examine the farmhouse grounds with that in mind. The operation failed to detect any trace of the toddler.

Four years later, however, in September 2016, Greek police informed Ben's family that an island resident had come forward with information. They said a builder who had been operating a digger at the farmhouse site on the day of Ben's disappearance had told him the child had died in an accident and he had hidden the body in waste from the site. The builder had since died of cancer, but a new police search was undertaken on the basis of this information, focused around a tree that had been planted since Ben had disappeared.

Any items of interest that were dug up among the more than 800 tons of soil excavated were sent to the UK for analysis. One of these, a yellow Dinky car, was identified by the Needham family as having been in Ben's possession when he went missing. This bolstered the belief of the detective inspector in charge of the inquiry that "Ben Needham died as a result of an accident near to the farmhouse in Iraklis where he was last seen playing". Detective Inspector Cousins went on, "The recovery of this item, and its location, further adds to my belief that material was removed from the farmhouse on or shortly after the day that Ben disappeared."

In 2017, traces of blood found on a sandal and on soil inside the toy car were tested to see if they matched Ben's DNA, but it was determined that they did not. The official line continued to be that Ben Needham was believed to have died in a tragic accident on the building site close to where he was last seen playing. However, without any physical evidence of remains after two excavations, the Needham family have always held on to the hope that Ben would eventually be found.

JUDGE JOSEPH CRATER: THE MISSINGEST MAN

When a 41-year-old judge vanished off the streets of Manhattan near Times Square in the summer of 1930, he was dubbed "the missingest man in New York". Nicknamed "Good Time Joe", Judge Joseph Crater was known for his affairs with showgirls as well as being suspected of corruption in his political aspirations. But his disappearance on the evening of 6 August 1930, after leaving a Midtown restaurant and getting into a cab, left everyone who knew him stumped, sparking one of the most talked about manhunts of the twentieth century.

Immediately prior to his disappearance, Crater had been holidaying with his wife in Maine. She claimed that he had been visibly upset by a mysterious phone call he had received during the trip and had then returned to New York early, saying he had to "straighten those fellows out", promising her he would be back within a week for her birthday.

At their Fifth Avenue apartment, he gave the maid a few days off. On the morning that he vanished, according to his secretary, he went through some personal files, destroyed a number of documents, and arranged for a substantial amount of money to be withdrawn from his bank account. He and his clerk carried two suitcases to his apartment, then he bought a theatre ticket, and went out for dinner at a chophouse with friends. He was believed to be heading for the theatre when he got into a cab.

Ten days after he'd left Maine, his wife started calling friends to ask if they'd seen him. But while she guessed he was still attending to whatever had brought him back to New York, business or pleasure, his friends and office assumed he had returned to Maine. He was not reported missing for four weeks, when he failed to show up in court on 25 August.

Once the news broke, it made the front page of every newspaper across the country, with sightings reported in every state and internationally as well. Dozens of theories were put forward as to what had happened to the dapper judge, including amnesia, suicide, running off with a showgirl, being "rubbed out" by the Mafia, expiring in the arms of a prostitute, failing to pay off a blackmailer – the list went on...

But of the more than 16,000 tips detectives received, not one was substantiated, and "pulling a Crater" entered the language as a term for vanishing without a trace.

At his wife's request, Crater was declared legally dead in 1939. Then in August 2005, 75 years after Judge Crater had "pulled a Crater", a handwritten letter marked "Do not open until my death" was found in a metal box by the granddaughter of a recently deceased elderly woman, Stella Ferrucci-Good. In it, she claimed that her late husband Robert Good, together with an NYPD cop named Charles Burns and the cop's cabby brother, Frank Burns, were responsible for Judge Crater's death. She added that Crater was buried in Coney Island, under the boardwalk near West Eighth Street – at the current site of the New York Aquarium, where police sources confirmed that the skeletal remains of five bodies had indeed been unearthed in the mid-1950s, long before technology existed to accurately identify human remains. There was nothing left; it was too late. And the reason for whatever happened was still a mystery.

Although his wife was reduced to poverty after Judge Crater's strange disappearance, she visited a bar in Greenwich Village every year on 6 August for the rest of her life and ordered two drinks, one of them for herself, saying, "Good luck Joe, wherever you are."

MALAYSIAN AIRLINES FLIGHT MH370: THE FISHERMAN AND THE FLOTSAM

A piece of flotsam used by a fisherman's wife as a washboard for five years turned out to be a vital clue in one of the greatest mysteries in recent aviation history.

Malaysian Airlines Flight MH370 was on a scheduled route north-east from Kuala Lumpur to Beijing on 8 March 2014. The last communication from the co-pilot Fariq Hamid to air traffic controllers in Malaysia as the plane crossed the Gulf of Thailand was reportedly, "All right, good night." Then, 40 minutes into the flight, its communication system was turned off. The Malaysian military detected an unidentified object on its radar heading west. Although radar contact with the aircraft was lost, satellite signals showed that it continued flying for nearly six more hours.

The aircraft, a Boeing 777 – which has an excellent safety record – disappeared with 227 passengers, most of them Chinese, and 12 crew on board. There was no distress signal, or any evidence of bad weather or technical problems. The search area, initially vast due to the unknown flight path, was narrowed down 16 days later to a remote part of the Indian Ocean 1,550 miles south-west of Australia, with no survivors thought to be likely. Scattered reports suggested sightings of a burning aircraft, a low-flying aircraft, and a crash.

The first piece of debris wasn't found for another 16 months, when part of a wing was discovered on a beach on the French island of Réunion in the western Indian Ocean, 2,300 miles from the search area. Further pieces of debris were found over the next 18 months in a similar area, on the shores of Tanzania, Mozambique, South Africa, Madagascar and Mauritius, two from the cabin interior, suggesting that the plane had broken up on impact rather than undergoing a controlled descent.

The search was called off in 2017, and it took another five years for the ersatz washboard to be discovered in a Madagascan fisherman's yard and found to be a crucial part of MH370. The debris had been washed up on shore after a tropical storm and the fisherman kept it in his yard with no clue as to what it was.

It turned out to be the aircraft's landing-gear door, and the fact that it was damaged on the inside led to the conclusion that the landing gear must have been down when the plane crashed into the sea. This answered the question as to whether there had been an active pilot until the moment of impact: clearly, there must have been. Prior to this discovery, one of the theories had been that a "mass hypoxia event" – an accident, fire or malfunction causing a loss of oxygen on board – had rendered the passengers and crew unconscious.

The landing gear would not be normally lowered in the event of an emergency landing on water, as it would increase the chances of catastrophe. A 2022 report by British engineer Richard Godfrey and Blaine Gibson, an American self-described "MH370 wreckage hunter", concluded that "the end of the flight was in a high-speed dive designed to ensure the aircraft broke up into as many pieces as possible" and that the undercarriage had been lowered in order to sink it as quickly as possible, both of which showed a "clear intent to hide the evidence of the crash".

In other words, according to these two investigators, the downing of MH370, with the loss of 239 lives, was a deliberate act. But why?

In March 2022, on the eighth anniversary of the disappearance of MH370, Ocean Infinity, a company using robotics technology to search the seabed, announced that it would resume its quest to find the missing aircraft in 2023 or 2024. The search for answers continues.

CONNIE CONVERSE: A SAD SWAN SONG

In August 1974, just days after her fiftieth birthday, Connie Converse, one of the first ever singer-songwriters (if not *the* first), drove off in her Volkswagen Beetle and was never seen or heard from again. Except, that is, through the legacy of her songs, which were largely unknown until they were featured on an American radio show in 2004, 30 years after she vanished.

Born Elizabeth Eaton Converse in Laconia, New Hampshire, in 1924, she was active as a musician in New York City in the 1950s, where she started using the name Connie. According to the music historian David Garland, "Everything we value in singer-songwriters today – personal perspective, insight, originality, empathy, intelligence, wry humour – was abundant in her music." Yet the idea of a singer-songwriter was still new, and she only made one public appearance.

Having been brought up in a strict Baptist family, Converse started drinking and smoking in New York, and possibly as a result, her parents rejected her music career and her father never heard her sing. In 1961, the year singer-songwriter Bob Dylan first moved to New York's Greenwich Village and quickly found mainstream success, Converse, frustrated with trying to sell her music there, relocated to Ann Arbor, Michigan, where she largely stopped writing songs and became a writer for and managing editor of *The Journal of Conflict Resolution*.

Her own inner conflict, however, left her burnt out and depressed, especially when in 1972 the journal's offices suddenly moved to Yale University in Connecticut. Trips to England and Alaska did nothing to lift her mood, and news that she needed a hysterectomy left her devastated.

In August 1974, Converse told her family of her intention to make a new life somewhere else, writing a letter saying, "Let me go. Let me be if I can. Let me not be if I can't... Human society fascinates me & awes me & fills me with grief & joy; I just can't find my place to plug into it." She also sent a letter to her brother enclosing a cheque to cover payment of her life insurance policy, but only up to a certain date.

By the time her family received her letters, she had packed her belongings in her Volkswagen Beetle and driven off, never to be heard from again.

A decade after Converse disappeared, her family hired a private investigator to find her; a few years previously, someone had told her brother that she'd seen the name Elizabeth Converse in a phone book in either Kansas or Oklahoma, a lead he hadn't followed up at the time. However, the investigator told the family that even if he found her, it was her right to disappear and he couldn't bring her back against her wishes. The family's attempts to locate her then ceased, though her brother suspected that she may have taken her own life by driving her car into a body of water.

It was Gene Deitch, the visual artist who had helped arrange her public appearance, who in 2004 played some basic recordings he'd made of Converse on David Garland's radio show *Spinning on Air*, sparking interest in her work. In 2015, an 18-track vinyl album was released of Converse's songs that she'd tried so hard to sell so many decades before, to no avail. The title of the album, *How Sad, How Lovely*, might also describe her life, her talent and her struggle for recognition and happiness, all of which seem to have come to an end in 1974, though what actually happened to Connie Converse will forever be cast in a shadow of doubt.

BISON DELE: NO WORRIES

When 30-year-old Bison Dele retired from his career as a professional National Basketball Association (NBA) player before the 1999–2000 season, he was still at the height of his game, with five years and $35.45 million remaining on his contract. He had other interests he wanted to devote his time to, though, and he'd made enough money from basketball to allow him to do so comfortably. Born Brian Carson Williams, he had changed his name to Bison Dele to honour his African and Cherokee heritage.

As well as playing various musical instruments, he had a pilot's licence. After retiring, he started spending longer periods travelling in the Mediterranean, East Asia and the wilds of Australia; he learned to sail and purchased a 55-foot catamaran. Early in 2002, Dele and his girlfriend, Serena Karlan, set sail for Auckland, New Zealand on the vessel, which he had named *Hakuna Matata* (Swahili for "No Worries"). He hired 32-year-old Frenchman Bertrand Saldo as skipper.

While they were in New Zealand, Dele's long-estranged older brother Miles Dabord arrived, wanting to reconnect with him. Relations still appeared to be strained, and on 29 May, the catamaran left Auckland for the French Polynesian island of

Tahiti, with only Dabord and the skipper on board. Dele and Karlan had decided to fly, and left the next day.

On 19 June, the boat arrived in Tahiti and Dabord was joined by Dele and Karlan, who had been staying in a luxury resort on Moorea, awaiting its arrival. On 6 July, the three of them set sail with Saldo for the island of Raiatea, from there planning to reach Hawaii. Three satellite phone calls were made from the boat on 8 July, but what happened afterwards is unknown. Dele and Karlan, who had previously kept in regular contact with their families, went silent. On 20 July, Dabord arrived back in Tahiti on the catamaran, alone.

On 5 September, he was arrested in Phoenix, Arizona after attempting to purchase $152,096 of Gold Eagle coins using Dele's name, bank account and passport. Apprehended by police, he claimed he was buying the gold on behalf of his brother, whom he told police was with Karlan in Tahiti. He was released after seven hours of questioning due to lack of evidence, and crossed the border into Mexico.

Meanwhile, a boat registered as the *Aria Bella* and docked on the south-east shore of Tahiti was found to be the repainted *Hakuna Matata*. Not only had its nameplate been removed, but what appeared to be bullet holes had been patched over.

At around the same time, Dabord, who had checked into a hotel in Tijuana, phoned his mother to tell her he would never hurt Dele and that he could not survive in prison.

It was enough for the police to move in, with the help of Dele's family and friends. Dabord was found half naked and comatose in Tijuana, and was taken to a California hospital. On 27 September, he died of an intentional insulin overdose.

So, what had happened to the others? It turned out that Dabord's girlfriend had heard a version of events from him.

Erica Wiese had joined him at a resort in Polynesia, believing at the time that Dele and Karlan were in Raiatea. However, eventually, Dabord told her that he and Dele had fought, and in the scuffle he had accidentally hit Karlan, whose head had then struck part of the boat, killing her. When the skipper wanted to report her death, Dele panicked and shot him. Dabord then said that he shot his brother in self-defence and threw the three bodies overboard before fleeing.

As everyone who had been on the boat at the time of the incident was now gone, no one would ever know. The FBI and French authorities concluded that Dele, Karlan and Saldo were indeed probably murdered by Dabord and then thrown overboard. No further investigations were carried out, and a memorial service was held for the brothers.

LORD LUCAN: THREE CARDS AND THE TRUTH

When Sandra Rivett was bludgeoned to death with a lead pipe on the evening of 7 November 1974 in the basement of the expensive London house where she was nanny to three children, the identity of her attacker was never in much doubt. Not just because of the three cards from the murder-mystery board game *Cluedo* (*Clue* in the US) allegedly left in the suspect's abandoned car – Colonel Mustard, Hallway and Lead Pipe – but also because the other person who was attacked that night identified the assailant as her husband, Richard John Bingham, more commonly known as Lord Lucan.

An aristocratic professional gambler once considered for the role of James Bond, by 1974, "Lucky Lucan", as he became known after a huge win in 1960, was in deep debt and involved in a bitter custody battle for his children. His wife, Veronica, had developed severe postnatal depression after the birth of each of their three children, and by 1973 the marriage had disintegrated, with Lucan moving out of the family home in Belgravia into a nearby flat. Hiring private investigators to spy on Veronica, he hoped to discredit her sufficiently to win custody of the children, but in June 1973, she was awarded full custody.

Lucan is reported to have told more than one person that he wanted to kill his wife in order to get his children and home back. If sold, the house would enable him to pay off his mounting debts. Lucan's behaviour became increasingly erratic and threatening over the next year, and by the time Rivett took up employment at the Belgravia house, a succession of nannies had come and gone, reporting strange interactions with Lucan.

On the night Rivett was murdered, Lucan contacted his mother, asking her to collect the children as there had been an incident. He claimed he had been passing the house when he saw his wife struggling with an unknown man. On entering, he went down to the basement and slipped in a pool of blood. The stranger fled and his wife became hysterical, accusing Lucan of hiring someone to murder her.

But Lady Lucan identified her husband as the attacker. When she went to find Rivett, she heard her husband's voice as he emerged from the basement. She then got into a fight with him, finally managing to escape when he went to get her a towel to wipe blood from her face.

By the time the police arrived, Lucan was long gone. He drove to a friend in Sussex, then the 7th Earl of Lucan disappeared. His car, with bloodstains matching those of both victims (together with, allegedly, the three incriminating playing cards) was found abandoned at the cross-Channel-ferry port of Newhaven.

Roy Ranson, the police chief in charge of the murder investigation, believed that Lucan had taken his own life. Lady Lucan, too, said that she thought her husband had killed himself "like the nobleman he was". However, with no body ever being found, Lucan's son, George Bingham, was unable to inherit his father's title until a death certificate was finally issued in 2016, when he became the 8th Earl of Lucan. Lady Lucan took her own life in 2017.

Over the decades, however, many claimed the missing Lucan faked his death and he's apparently been spotted in India, New Zealand, Gabon and Australia. The latter was near Brisbane, where a man the same age as Lucan was found by Rivett's son in 2020. The elderly man was apparently positively identified by state-of-the-art facial recognition technology as "Lucky Lucan". It seems, however, that the man in question is still to be found. So, will the mystery ever be solved?

GHOSTS AND HAUNTINGS

We hope that when we die, our souls will rest in peace.

But perhaps, depending on the circumstances of our death, some of us are bound to linger somewhere between life and death, seeking resolution to an untimely end, even attempting to exact revenge from beyond the grave on those responsible for our demise.

Whether you believe that or not, there are some phenomena that simply cannot find explanations in science. Or as Shakespeare put it in one of his most famous plays starring a ghost, "There are more things in heaven and earth, Horatio, than are dreamt of in your philosophy."

And the success of ghost tours, haunted houses and even holidays where you're guaranteed to be kept awake by other-worldly presences proves that we're all suckers for a spooky story.

Naturally, it's usually very old buildings that are said to be haunted – medieval castles being a favourite. Yet the Old Changi Hospital in Singapore, built in the 1930s, is said to be as alive with apparitions as the ancient English Ram Inn.

As you'll read in this chapter, there's not a corner of the world that's untouched by traumatized souls unable to completely shed their mortal coil, from ghostly galloping horses to thespians whose final curtain call has never ended. Grey ladies and black dogs seem particularly prone to running down creepy corridors for eternity.

Can they all just be a figment of the imagination? Read on to find out...

CATACOMBS OF PARIS: "DON'T SEARCH"

It's perhaps not surprising that a vast network of tunnels lined with bones and skulls should be the source of many chilling stories.

The Catacombs of Paris date to the late eighteenth century, shortly before the French Revolution, when the city's overcrowded cemeteries were linked to public health problems. A new site was chosen in an area that was then outside Paris. Bones were exhumed, transported at night and dumped in the labyrinthine abandoned quarries. Eventually the bones were arranged into walls and the Paris Catacombs were opened to the public in 1809.

Its eerie depths, subterranean home to 6 million corpses, 20 yards below the city's bustling boulevards and with 200 miles of tunnels, are certainly no place to get lost.

Legend has it that anyone who finds themselves inside the creepy charnel house after midnight will hear ghostly voices coming from the walls, urging them to go deeper and deeper in, until eventually they get so disorientated they can't find their way out.

This shocking fate is thought to have befallen a doorman at the Val-de-Grâce hospital – where Benedictine nuns were caring for the injured of the Revolution – in 1793. It's believed that 61-year-old Philibert Aspairt may have strayed mistakenly into the Catacombs' tunnels while heading for the wine cellar, possibly also somewhat the worse for a drink or two himself. Carrying just a candle to find his way, perhaps he became irretrievably lost when the flame went out. All that is known for certain is that 11 years later, his body was found deep inside, identifiable from the hospital key still hanging round his neck. He was buried where he died, and every year on 3 November, his ghost is said to haunt the tunnels that lured him to his death.

Two centuries later, in the early 1990s, a similar mysterious fate may have befallen an unknown cameraman, whose video footage was found still in his camera by a group exploring the maze-like ossuary. If it is genuine, then it is perhaps even more chilling since his voice spoke to them through the recording. From the film and its soundtrack, it was evident that the man had become lost and, with no idea how to get out, grew increasingly frantic with terror. Eventually he dropped the camera, and that's where the film cut out. To this day, his identity and his ultimate fate remain unknown.

The Catacombs were host to a Nazi bunker and a Resistance shelter during the Second World War. There are secret entrances through basements and Metro lines. Only a small area of the Catacombs is open to the public given that some of the galleries are unsafe, yet every year on Halloween, people risk the fines and dangers and descend into the prohibited areas.

And an anonymous warning given to a group of police officers exploring the Catacombs in 2004 remains an unsolved mystery. The gendarmes made the bizarre discovery of a vast area of subterranean galleries wired illegally for phones, with a bar, a lounge, and even a cinema. On the ceiling, they found live cameras recording their every move. When they brought a larger team in a few days later to investigate further, everything had vanished.

All that was there now was a piece of paper with a brief but ominous note written on it: *Ne cherchez pas* (Don't search)…

PANDEMIC HAUNTINGS: THINGS THAT GO BUMP IN LOCKDOWN

Confined to their homes by the Covid-19 pandemic, many people found that they were not as alone as they first thought. And it wasn't just Zoom meetings and schooling the kids at home that provided the extra company. Ghosts, poltergeists and other supernatural presences suddenly made themselves known too...

For IT expert Adrian Gomez, aged 26, and his partner, both of whom worked remotely from their Los Angeles apartment for the duration of lockdown, which started in March 2020, things started out quietly enough. But by mid-April, they couldn't ignore the persistent yet inexplicable noises and activity around their living space – rattling doorknobs, shaking window shades, and footsteps up above them, where nobody lived.

"I'm a fairly rational person," said Gomez. "I try to think, 'What are the reasonable, tangible things that could be causing this?' But when I don't have those answers, I start to think, 'Maybe something else is going on.'"

They were by no means the only ones to have paranormal experiences during the pandemic. Across the globe, reports of ghostly sightings shot up as lockdown took effect. Andy Wilson of Paranormal Research Investigators UK claimed to have received as many as three times more enquiries during the pandemic.

"We did see an increase in cases reporting poltergeist-type activity from the full range of the social spectrum, for example, the unemployed, retired nurses, lawyers, ex-special forces," he said.

At the Shrubbery Hotel in Ilminster, Somerset, footsteps and voices were heard, and people felt their hair being pulled. When the hotel – built in the 1850s but on a much older site in an area known for Civil War activity – conducted a paranormal investigation, the manager reported sightings of a "cavalier" figure in the dining room and a sensation of being touched in the kitchen and cellar. But was this just a publicity stunt by the Best Western-owned hotel, which has a page on its website dedicated to haunted hotels?

Yet Marc Wahlberg and his son Zachary in Oldham, Greater Manchester, reported shadowy figures and strange smells accompanied by objects mysteriously going missing over the course of the two years of lockdown. They heard footsteps in an empty room – which their dogs avoided and sometimes growled at.

In the US, before strict stay-at-home restrictions were in force, Patrick Hinds, together with his partner and daughter, rented an Airbnb cottage in Western Massachusetts where, one morning in the early hours, Hinds walked into the kitchen for a drink and saw a soldier from the Second World War sitting at the table.

"It seemed normal in the split second before I realized, wait, what's happening? And as I turned to look, he was gone," said Hinds. "It didn't feel menacing at all."

For those who believe in ghosts, there's a logical explanation for the rise in sightings during the pandemic: the increased tension that would naturally result from the living occupants suddenly spending a lot more time in places that the ghosts had previously had to themselves for much of the day.

On the other hand, for the more pragmatic, there's a rather more mundane explanation. John E. L. Tenney, a paranormal researcher and the former host of the US TV show *Ghost Stalkers*, believes many of the strange noises that people were hearing could be easily accounted for. "When the sun comes up and the house starts to warm up, they're usually at work – they're not used to hearing the bricks pop and the wood expand. It's not that the house wasn't making those sounds. They just never had the time to notice it."

But the sightings and moving objects are perhaps another matter.

THE GHOSTS OF MONTE CRISTO

In 1963, a couple purchased a decrepit old mansion house on a hill overlooking Junee, a small town in the Riverina region of New South Wales, Australia, for a mere £1,000. They thought they were getting a bargain, given that the property, which had been empty since 1948, included the former servants' quarters, a dairy, a stable block, a ballroom and acres of land. But when they set about restoring the Monte Cristo Homestead to its former glory, strange things started happening. The property has since become known as Australia's most haunted house...

First of all, their dog and cat didn't want to go into the house. Then late one evening, on returning from a trip to buy building supplies, Olive and Reginald Ryan were astonished to see bright lights blazing from every window of the wreck which, at that point, had no electricity. Convinced burglars must be inside, they told their children to stay in the car while they went to investigate. But as they approached the house, the lights all vanished – and no one was found inside.

Although the incident was unnerving, it didn't stop the Ryans from completing their renovation of the property and then moving in – only to experience many more inexplicable events once they were living there. They often heard footsteps walking across an upstairs balcony and glimpsed a woman in white standing on it. Olive felt invisible hands resting on her shoulders, and heard her name being called. Heavy pictures dropped off the walls but remained intact.

Then, one evening, one of their daughters went to check on her little brother, Lawrence, who had gone to bed – only to see an elderly man dressed in old-fashioned clothes standing at the end of the bed. No one was found in the bedroom on further investigation, but when he was a teenager, Lawrence moved into a different bedroom, saying ominously, "I always felt like someone was watching me in that room."

The elegant, prestigious house had been built in late Victorian style in 1885 by Christopher William Crawley, once a struggling farmer who had wisely bought some land and made his wealth after the opening of the railway. He lived there with his family and servants until his death at 69. His wife became a recluse on his death, and continued to live there – spending most of her time in the attic where she had built a chapel – until she died at 92. However, two of their servants and one of their children met far more untimely ends. What happened behind Monte Cristo's doors?

A young maid is said to have fallen to her death from the balcony, the bleach stain from attempts to remove the spilled blood still being visible. She was rumoured to have been pregnant, fuelling speculation that the fall may not have been an accident. Likewise, a stable boy died from burns suffered when his straw mattress was set on fire. The saying that bad luck comes in threes held true at the Monte Cristo Homestead, when the nanny dropped the baby granddaughter down the stairs – perhaps not accidentally.

With at least three people having died in suspicious circumstances at the property during its late-nineteenth-century heyday, the apparitions and strange noises would certainly suggest to some the presence of spirits. Since 1993, Lawrence Ryan has openly embraced the troubled past of the home where he grew up, offering ghoulish bed-and-breakfast stays and ghost tours to visitors from all over the world, some of whom claim to have had paranormal experiences during their haunted-house holiday.

THE EVIL JAN TREGEAGLE

The legendary Cornish demon Jan Tregeagle is thought to have started out as a real flesh-and-blood person – one whose evil ways resulted in the forever restless creature he turned into on his demise. The dastardly deeds he committed as an unscrupulously harsh magistrate in early-seventeenth-century Bodmin led, they say, to the perpetual wandering ways of Tregeagle's wild spirit, whose ghostly wailing reverberates along the rugged coastline and echoes across the bleak moorland of Cornwall in the far south-west of England. According to some stories, he may have murdered his wife, made a pact with the Devil and cheated an orphan of their inheritance.

Having a belated sense of remorse on his deathbed at how thoroughly evil he had been during his life, however, he enlisted the help of the church – pouring money into their coffers helped in this regard – in saving his soul. Constant prayer and exorcisms followed, and on Tregeagle's death, he was buried in a church graveyard near the town of Wadebridge. But the demons wouldn't let him off so easily. So, as a gaunt, shadowy ghost, Tregeagle put in an appearance at an important trial where an innocent man was about to be convicted. The defendant called upon one final witness, Tregeagle (others say the defendant said, "If Tregeagle ever saw it, I wish to God he would come and declare it!"). The ghost of Tregeagle appeared in the witness box, was questioned by the judge, and testified to his own forgery, proving that the man was not guilty.

But having come back from the grave, Tregeagle was once again in danger from the demons. That was when his eternal fate was decided once and for all at a lengthy conference presided over by the Prior of Bodmin. Because of the good deed he had just done in the courtroom, they would keep his spirit busy with an impossible task, thus out of reach of the demons and hounds of hell until his hoped-for salvation on Judgement Day.

The task was to empty out the water of the gloomy lake known as Dozmary Pool on Bodmin Moor, using only a limpet shell with a hole in it. If he should ever cease work on the task, even for a moment, the demons would leap on him and drag him down with them to hell. He set to it in earnest, but needless to say there came a moment when he paused, and the demons came chasing. There followed a lively pursuit, but finally he escaped and was given another task, and then another...

The spirit of Tregeagle is today near Land's End, sweeping the sand from Porthcurno Cove round the headland of Tol-Pedn-Penwith into Nanjizal (or Mill) Bay. Legend has it – and anyone who knows that wild part of Cornwall will vouch for it too – that on many a winter's night, the ghost can be heard howling and roaring at the hopelessness of his task.

HAMPTON COURT PALACE: RAUCOUS ROYALS

Hampton Court Palace outside London, a British treasure with 1,390 rooms, was built by Cardinal Wolsey but so adored by King Henry VIII that he acquired it in 1528, and brought all six of his wives there at one point or another. Apparently, at least two of them remain there to this day – or rather, their troubled ghosts do...

Once a year, a pale, sad, wraith-like figure is said to appear on the Silverstick Stairs, carrying a lighted candle. It is thought to be his beloved third wife, the quiet and retiring Jane Seymour, whom Henry regarded as his "perfect" queen. Tragically, she died of complications two weeks after giving birth to his longed-for only son, Edward, at Hampton Court in 1537, leaving Henry devastated, but also leaving her lingering presence on the staircase outside the birthing room. It is said she appears on the anniversary of Edward's birth in October.

The ghost of Henry's fifth wife, Catherine Howard, is much noisier and more often sighted. In life, Catherine was wild and exuberant, and in 1542, when she was just 19, Henry accused her of adultery and treason. On her arrest at Hampton Court, she is said to have fled from the guards in terror, and to have run through a hall, screaming out to Henry for mercy. Her screams were in vain. She was dragged away to be beheaded at the Tower of London. Her traumatized ghost is said to have remained in what is now called the Haunted Gallery, screaming forever.

Another frequent apparition at Hampton Court is the "Grey Lady", believed by many to be the ghost of Sybil Penn, who served as a nurse both to Edward VI (Jane Seymour's son) and to the future Queen Elizabeth I, Henry's daughter by his second wife, Anne Boleyn. In 1562, Sybil nursed Elizabeth through smallpox but then caught it herself and died soon after. She was buried in nearby Hampton Church, but sightings of the Grey Lady began after the church was renovated in 1829, disturbing her tomb. Sybil is also known to have spun wool, and in 1871, when a wall was knocked down in an apartment at Hampton Court, an old, well-used spinning wheel was found – at which point the spinning noises that one resident had heard frequently up until then suddenly stopped.

Also in 1871, during an excavation of the cloister in Fountain Court, two male skeletons were unearthed. They are thought to have been Civil War Royalists put to death by the Roundheads and buried in unmarked graves. The resident of a "grace and favour" apartment, whom no one had previously believed when she complained of knocking and banging noises in the walls, put it succinctly when she said afterwards, "That stupid board of works has at last found the two wretched men... who have been haunting me for years." After they were properly buried, the strange sounds stopped.

Many ghostly encounters have been reported, such as the time staff were preparing for a function in the Queen's gallery when they heard a door opening and footsteps, or when two

American visitors were found shaking with fear after seeing a headless figure believed to be Anne Boleyn. And one ghostly apparition was even caught on CCTV in October 2003. The footage can still be viewed on the internet of a figure dressed in what looks very much like a Tudor-era cloak flinging open, and then pulling shut, a fire door. But whether the spooky doorperson is clear evidence of a ghost or merely a convincing hoax, no one, to this day, has been able to say.

AMITYVILLE HORROR HOUSE

For the first 47 years of its existence, nothing untoward happened at 112 Ocean Avenue, a five-bedroom, three-bathroom Dutch colonial-style house in the town of Amityville, New York. On the night of 13 November 1974, however, six members of the DeFeo family were murdered there as they slept in their beds by the seventh member of the family, 24-year-old Ronald DeFeo Jr. Using a .35-calibre Marlin rifle, he took 15 minutes to shoot his entire family dead, after which he showered and went to the local bar, hysterically shouting that someone had killed his family.

Although he initially told police that a Mafia hitman had shot his family and then held a gun to his head, he eventually confessed that he was the murderer, saying, "Once I started, I just couldn't stop. It went so fast." He pleaded insanity, saying he'd heard his family's voices in his head plotting against him, but was convicted of second-degree murder and received six life sentences. In 2021, 47 years after the murders, he died.

When the house was put on the market more than a year after the killings, priced very low, the buyers, the Lutz family, were unaware of its history, and paid an extra $400 for the furniture to be included in the sale. But within a month, the

Lutzes had moved out, terrified by what they said had started happening almost immediately on their arrival.

Mr and Mrs Lutz – George and Kathy – claimed to have seen a demon with half its head blown off, as well as green slime oozing down the walls in the hall. George woke at 3.15 every morning – the exact time of the killings – and he also kept being woken by the sound of the front door slamming, though no one else heard it and the front door was always closed when he checked it. Kathy had recurring nightmares about the murders and said she felt herself "being embraced" by an unseen force. Their daughter Missy befriended a demonic red-eyed pig she claimed to see, which she called Jodie. A crucifix on the wall kept turning upside down, and giant cloven hoofprints appeared in the snow outside the house on New Year's Day.

When they asked a priest to bless the house, he claimed to hear a loud masculine voice telling him to "get out" as soon as he started to splash holy water inside. He said that he subsequently developed a high fever and that his palms became blistered with marks similar to a stigmata – the wound on the hands of Christ from being nailed to the cross.

The Lutzes moved out, never to return, but sold their story to writer Jay Anson, who in 1977 published the multi-million-copy bestseller *The Amityville Horror: A True Story*, which spawned 16 *Amityville* horror movies. Although dubbed a true story, containing much factual information and based on hours of interviews with the Lutzes, the book was fictionalized. The new owners of the house, the Cromarty family, refuted claims that they had experienced similar horrors there, saying, "The quiet village of Amityville, Long Island, has been made infamous by a hoax. It will possibly never be the same. It is

Long Island's equivalent to Watergate." They blamed the book's publisher and author for giving "credibility to two liars, and allow[ing] them the privilege of putting the word true on a book which in all actuality is a novel".

Whatever the reality is, the windows on the top floor that looked like demonic eyes were replaced with less emotive ones, and the address 112 Ocean Avenue no longer exists. It is now 108 Ocean Avenue…

GHOSTS OF GOOD HOPE

At Cape Town's seventeenth-century Castle of Good Hope, the bell in the tower sometimes rings of its own accord. It's just one of many strange occurrences in the fortress, South Africa's oldest surviving colonial building and perhaps one of its most haunted. Could it be the ghost of a soldier who is said to have hanged himself by the bell-rope?

It's said that those who guard the castle at night are afraid of the restless souls in the building. Regularly reported apparitions include a vicious black dog that lunges at people before suddenly vanishing, and some have seen a tall man jump from the castle walls but disappear before reaching the ground.

Built between 1666 and 1679 by the Dutch East India Company using slaves, soldiers and sailors as the workforce, the pentagonal bastion fort has a church, a bakery, living quarters, shops and cells. It was built on the shores of Table Bay, originally as a refreshment base for ships plying the spice route to East Asia and was also used as protection from attack by the English fleet at a time of hostility between the two nations.

It is said that Governor Pieter Gijsbert van Noodt had a curse placed on him after he refused to grant a final wish to a prisoner he had condemned to death on 23 April 1728. Later on the day of the hanging, van Noodt, who had been in good health that morning, was found dead in his office, having had a fatal heart attack. His embittered ghost is regularly heard, by staff and visitors alike, cursing and swearing inside the castle walls.

Another of the castle's ghostly occupants, Lady Anne Barnard, lived there as "first lady" from 1797 and in the governor's absence was responsible for entertaining official visitors. Said to have been an attractive woman in her forties who constructed the Dolphin Pool at the castle and bathed nude there, she also recorded her time at the Cape Colony in journals and spent three years painting a seven-sectioned panoramic view of the city from the castle, which now hangs in her family's ancestral home in Scotland. It seems she was a strong personality who loved her five years at the Cape, and perhaps that's why people claim to have seen Lady Anne's spirit still making its presence known when VIPs visit.

Surely the scariest part of the castle, though, is its windowless dungeon, called Donker Gat or "Dark Hole", which was also used as a torture chamber, with convicts being chained to the walls. During floods, the water rose quickly. When the castle was used as a prison during the Second Boer War from 1899 to 1902, the dungeon sometimes flooded, drowning its captive occupants. The first inkling of any paranormal activity was a few years later, in 1915, when a tall male figure – deemed to be an apparition – was seen jumping off one of the castle walls and then walking between two of its buttresses. People still report hearing voices and footsteps in the dungeon as well as the narrow corridors. Maintenance work on the fortress has revealed rooms that had been bricked up, and architects believe others must exist.

GHOSTS AND HAUNTINGS

The Castle of Good Hope had its share of dark events including a Lady in Grey, who often used to be spotted running through the castle in hysterical tears, but this no longer occurred after a female skeleton was unearthed during an excavation in the castle grounds.

THE HELLFIRE CLUB

The imposing, dark grey, stone walls of the abandoned "Hellfire Club" stand in a clearing on wooded Montpelier Hill above Dublin, Ireland, remarkably intact except for its gaping windows. It was built in 1725 as a hunting club, though its structure is reminiscent of a church, and it has long been linked with stories of supernatural happenings connected to satanic rituals.

The very stones from which the club was built are thought by some to have been the reason for its rocky start. The Irish Speaker of the Commons and landowner William Conolly had taken them from a prehistoric cairn that had stood above a passage grave. Shortly after the building was completed, its roof was blown off in a storm. Could it be, as some thought, that spirits were venting their fury on Conolly for desecrating the ancient burial site?

It was after Conolly's death that the place became the venue for the Hellfire Club. The club had been founded by Richard Parsons, who was said to have dabbled in black magic. Many Hellfire clubs sprang up during the seventeenth and eighteenth centuries across Britain and Ireland, with the Devil appointed as their president. From that point on, the building was believed to be a place of illicit activities, some simply decadent or debauched, involving sex and alcohol, and some violent, even including murder, opening the door to the succession of spirits said to haunt it to this day.

One night a young farmer is said to have seen more than he bargained for when he was invited to witness the club's activities. The following morning, he was found trembling and scared out of his wits, and he is thought never to have uttered a single word again. What could he have seen?

Perhaps it's related to the famous story that tells of its members playing cards one stormy night when a cloaked stranger came by looking for shelter. He was invited inside and joined in the card game. When, later in the evening, someone bent down to pick up a card they had dropped, they glimpsed a cloven hoof sticking out from beneath the stranger's cloak, revealing him to be the Devil. His cover blown, the Devil set the club on fire, leaving it in the ruined state it remains in today.

Others say the fire started when someone spilled a drink on a member's cloak, the ensuing flames taking several victims and putting an end to the Hellfire Club's activities. But then the next generation revived it as "The Holy Fathers", with more evil rituals and general hellraising.

Another creepy legend associated with the club tells of a priest hurriedly performing an exorcism on a black cat that was being sacrificed, in the hope of preventing an evil spirit being released from the cat's dead body. When Killakee House, another hunting lodge nearby, was being converted, it became renowned for a ghostly black cat that left several tradesmen haunted by the sight of its glowing red eyes. Others believe that was the spirit of yet another poor feline, doused in whisky and set alight by the Hellfire Club members in Killakee House. Whatever the case, both buildings remain linked to satanic cults and unexplained supernatural events.

A PLAGUE OF GHOSTS

A tiny, low-lying, tree-filled island close to Venice has been abandoned for over half a century. With its prime location off one of Italy's most alluring destinations, entrepreneurs have been tempted to develop it for luxury hotels and recreation, but then pulled out. Though nobody lives there, disembodied voices and screams are often reportedly heard, and dark, fleeting shadows flit past. Poveglia has the nickname "Island of Ghosts".

Set in the lagoon between Venice and the Lido, the small island was first mentioned in chronicles dating back to 421 CE, when the citizens of Padua and Este fled there to escape the barbarian invasions. Its population grew steadily until it came under attack from a fleet from the rival city of Genoa in 1379, when it was abandoned. That's when its history became rather more morbid.

In the late eighteenth century the Public Health Office took it over to use as a checkpoint for ships entering the city. The plague epidemic that had begun centuries earlier had broken out in another wave, and after cases were discovered on some vessels, the island became a lazaretto to isolate the infected. From 1793 to 1814, anyone showing symptoms of the plague was forcibly taken to the quarantine station of Poveglia. When they died, they were cremated on mass pyres in an effort to stop the spread of the virulent disease. With 160,000 people estimated to have died of the plague there, it's no mystery why the island is thought to be haunted. To this day, the island's soil is said to contain more than 50 per cent human ash, adding to the eerie aura.

But the ghosts of plague victims are not the only ones to haunt the island. A mental asylum was later built there, and in the 1920s, an evil doctor is said to have conducted gruesome experiments, including lobotomies, on the patients. Sometime in the following decade, driven mad by the ghosts of his victims coming back to haunt him, he is said to have thrown himself off the bell tower, which was duly demolished, though residents living nearby claimed to still hear the bell ringing. Restoration work on the bell tower was started more recently, but it stopped abruptly, with no explanation being given.

The asylum closed in 1968, but the "Reparto Psichiatria" sign is still visible among the derelict buildings and discarded beds and baths, left for nature to take over. There is a government ban on anyone visiting Poveglia, though few would be keen to set foot on an island with such a gruesome past. Even local taxi drivers and fishermen steer well clear of the island whose dark, oppressive forces seem to reverberate into the present, and where the waters that surround it are still said to be full of rotting human remains.

WAS LIZZIE BUSY WITH AN AXE?

A neat and respectable-looking bed and breakfast at 230 Second Street, Fall River, Massachusetts came second in a rating of the ten most haunted hotels in the world, receiving an impressive 9.73 out of ten. The scene of a brutal double murder in 1892, it is known as the Lizzie Borden House.

Andrew Borden, its owner from 1872 to 1892, was of English and Welsh descent and although from a modest background, through various successful business ventures built a fortune. His children, Lizzie and Emma, had a religious upbringing and Lizzie was deeply involved in church groups and charitable work. When their mother died and Andrew married Abby, the relationship with Andrew's daughters became strained. Lizzie believed Abby was financially motivated and tension grew, with a family argument distancing them enough that at one point Lizzie stayed in a rooming house for a few days.

It was mid-morning on 4 August 1892 when Andrew and Abby Borden were savagely attacked inside their home and killed with multiple fierce blows to their heads with a hatchet; Abby first, and then Andrew. Lizzie, aged 32, was accused of the double murder, the trial causing a sensation across the US.

The details of the day are well documented. The investigating officers found Lizzie's attitude strangely cool, and after being informed that she was a suspect, the next day she was found by a friend tearing up a dress to put on the fire as it was apparently covered in paint...

Lizzie was acquitted, however, by an all-male jury who seemingly found it impossible to think that an upstanding Christian woman could have done such a thing. She and her sister moved to a house on French Street known as Maplecroft and inherited their father's fortune. Yet nobody else was found guilty of the murders and Lizzie lived under a cloud of suspicion for the rest of her life, becoming immortalized in a jaunty children's rhyme:

Lizzie Borden took an axe,
And gave her mother forty whacks;
When she saw what she had done,
She gave her father forty-one.

Martha McGinn, whose grandparents bought the house in 1948, opened it as a bed and breakfast in the late 1990s. The unsolved case remains sufficiently intriguing for the murder scene to attract a constant stream of curious visitors, many of whom claim that the house is haunted. And it's not just Andrew and Abby Borden whose spirits remain trapped. Lizzie herself is said to put in an appearance every so often – though she's apparently a busy Lizzie, also making her ghostly presence felt at Maplecroft. Two children murdered by their mother at a neighbouring house in 1848 are also said to come knocking sometimes.

Doors are said to open and close by themselves, accompanied by a floral scent. From creaking noises and freaky footsteps to children's laughter and spooky faces, there is a long list of unexplained occurrences at the Lizzie Borden House – including a tour guide's claim of being punched in the back by Andrew's ghost.

Others have a more down-to-earth view. One former tour guide said, "I've slept in the house alone, in every room, on every floor. I've never seen anything." She added that the odd sounds are mostly explainable; for example, the installation of air conditioning left holes in the old building so that noises can travel strangely.

The ghoulish presences many feel on visiting the house may simply be a reaction to the grisly nature of the murders that took place – as well as the mystery about what really happened that day back in 1892.

EXIT, PURSUED BY A GHOST

London's West End is replete with theatres, many of them with the reputation for being haunted. And it's not just thespians with overactive imaginations who've been spooked in these venerable old buildings – audience members, too, have seen their fair share of spectral scenes. The Lyceum Theatre's macabre severed head is thought to have belonged to a member of the family whose land the theatre was built on 200 years ago, and who was beheaded for treason. One evening, a couple sitting in the balcony claimed to have seen the creepy cranium staring up at them from the lap of a lady seated in the stalls below.

The Theatre Royal of Drury Lane, originally built in 1663, is not only one of London's oldest, but also, unsurprisingly, one of the most haunted. A famous Drury Lane ghost is the "Man in Grey", named after the grey cape he wears over his eighteenth-century-style clothing. Although seeing the Man in Grey appear in the shadows during rehearsals is said to be a good omen for a play's success, the man may have had less good luck in his own life if his was the skeleton covered in grey rags that was uncovered during renovations in the 1840s, thought to belong to someone who was stabbed to death.

The ghost of another unlucky man is also said to roam the Drury Lane Theatre's passages and stage: Irish actor Charles

Macklin, who in 1735 got into a dispute with another actor for a wig while they were rehearsing for the play *Trick for Trick*. When the argument escalated into a physical fight, he lunged at the other man with a stick – which penetrated the actor's eye and then his brain, killing him. The death was deemed an accident but apparently traumatized by this freak fatality, Macklin's spirit appears forever bound to haunt the theatre.

A scented spectre is also well-known at the Drury Lane Theatre. Actor and comedian Dan Leno died at the age of 43 in 1904, but the lavender fragrance he was fond of using has continued to waft around the theatre. His invisible, mischievous presence is also said to be responsible for pushing actors off the stage every now and then.

But the last word must go to William Terris, an actor-manager who was enjoying a successful run in the play *Secret Service* at the Adelphi Theatre in 1897 when he was stabbed to death at the stage door by a jealous former friend and minor actor. Terris' dying words – apparently in the arms of his lover, the leading lady – were, "I will be back." Judging by the spooky sightings and other inexplicable events and noises that have been reported at the theatre ever since, including knocks at the dressing-room door that once belonged to the leading lady, he was true to his word.

GREAT BALLS OF FIRE

A ball of fire rushes along the railway track then vanishes as you approach it; an invisible child wails for his mother, a pitiful cry that goes forever unanswered; and a phantom army marches forever through town. Little Harpers Ferry, one of the most historical towns in the US state of West Virginia, is also one of the most haunted.

As its name would suggest, the little town originated around the confluence of the Potomac and Shenandoah rivers, a strategic location amid tree-covered hills, and in 1798, troops were sent there to prepare for a war with France. While they waited to be sent into action, however, cholera swept through the ranks, and many of the soldiers died – though there were no battle losses as the war never happened. The troops' spirits make their presence known to this day, still parading through the town bearing muskets and drums.

Harpers Ferry was also the setting for one of the earliest raids in the American Civil War. In 1859, John Brown, who was vehemently opposed to slavery, made a valiant attempt to take over the town's significant arsenal of weapons along with a band of fighters that included his two sons, three free Black men, one freed slave and a fugitive slave. He was defeated, with only five of his men escaping with their lives. Brown was executed afterwards, but his action became a pivotal one in the war, and his ghostly figure is regularly seen walking along the streets of Harpers Ferry by night, acknowledging anyone who notices him. Some have tried to photograph themselves next to John Brown's genial ghost, but only a blank space remains.

The sound of the little boy calling out for his mother is said to be the ghostly cry of a drummer boy who was tossed heartlessly out of a window by a Union soldier during the Civil War. During that time, St Peter's Catholic Church was used as a hospital in Harpers Ferry, and some say the priest's ghost can sometimes be seen praying for his town.

Are these ghostly shapes explainable by natural phenomena such as river mist and wildlife – or have the spirits remained to remind us of what happened? Shirley Dougherty opened a restaurant in Harpers Ferry in 1968, and although no believer in ghosts at the time, she soon had a few encounters with apparitions and started to research what had happened in the area, eventually publishing a book of the stories.

Perhaps the most chilling Harpers Ferry ghost story, that of "Screaming Jenny", relates not to a soldier, but to a kind-hearted homeless woman who lived in one of the abandoned storage sheds close to the railway tracks. One late-autumn evening, Jenny's heavy woollen skirt caught light while she was warming herself by a fire. The burning woman ran screaming towards the station for help but as her body became engulfed by flames, she strayed onto the tracks and was hit and killed by an oncoming train. She was given a pauper's funeral. Dead and buried, Jenny seemed quickly forgotten – until a month later.

On rounding the bend to Harpers Ferry station, another train ploughed into a screaming ball of fire, in a virtually identical incident. When the engineer brought the train to a halt and ran back to search for the body he was convinced the train had just hit, however, he found nothing – not even any scorch marks on the track. On being told what had happened, the stationmaster realized that Jenny's ghost had returned to haunt the spot where she had died. And, indeed, Jenny's phantom is said to appear as a fireball on the railway tracks each year on the anniversary of her horrific death, vanishing only when a train comes along and hits it.

ROYAL CALCUTTA GHOSTLY GALLOP

"Pride" was a pearl-white champion racehorse in 1930s India, the darling of her owner, George Williams, for whom she won race after race, making him a rich man.

In time, inevitably, Pride, who had been known in her heyday as the "Queen of the Tracks", grew old and frail, and the day after she lost the Annual Calcutta Derby, which had been due to be her last race, she was found dead on the racecourse of the Royal Calcutta Turf Club, in what is now Kolkata. Whether it was her despondent owner who ended her life, having lost his fortune when she lost the race, or whether she simply expired from the disappointment and shame of finally losing, no one will ever know.

But on moonlit Saturday nights, a ghostly white horse is sometimes seen by racegoers and maintenance staff to thunder past the stands. It has become known as Shaheb er Shada Ghora – "Sir's White Horse" – seemingly forever bound to gallop along the course where she both achieved glory and met her sad end.

THE FEMALE STRANGER

The US city of Alexandria, now in Virginia, lies on the Potomac River, and in the autumn of 1816, when it was a substantial port, a passing ship arriving from the Caribbean made a detour to drop off a couple of strangers. The woman, who wore a long, black veil to hide her face, was gravely ill.

Her husband took her by carriage to the City Hotel but refused to give their names. He then hired a doctor and nurses to care for his wife but made them swear not to reveal her identity if they became aware of it, or his, so the legend goes. The woman died three weeks after their arrival, and her husband arranged for her to be buried in the local cemetery of St Paul's. Even the elaborate inscription engraved on her tombstone – presumably at great expense, given its length – kept the secret of who she was, reading:

To the memory of a FEMALE STRANGER whose mortal sufferings terminated on the 14th day of October 1816
    Aged 23 years and 8 months
    This stone is placed here by her disconsolate
    Husband in whose arms she sighed out her latest breath and who under God did his utmost even to soothe the cold dead ear of death

How loved how valued once avails thee not
To whom related or by whom begot
A heap of dust alone remains of thee
Tis all thou art and all the proud shall be
To him gave all the Prophets witness that through his name
whosoever believeth in him shall receive remission of sins

The man borrowed a considerable amount of money for the tombstone and the plot from a local merchant. And then he disappeared, without settling any of the numerous bills he'd racked up during his wife's illness and demise, from the hotel room and medical care to the funeral. But because he had sworn everyone to secrecy, they could never identify him to the police as being the con man who well and truly stiffed them.

It may sound like a piece of elaborate fiction with a clever twist at the end, but the tombstone of the "female stranger" is there for all to see in St Paul's Cemetery, in the Old Town district of Alexandria, Virginia. The City Hotel, where the anonymous woman died, later became Gadsby's Tavern and still exists. And, according to some, so too does the female stranger's ghost...

On her first evening working as a waitress at Gadsby's, a young student, her arms laden with plates of food, turned out of the kitchen to go into the restaurant, only to see the female stranger staring directly at her. As the ghostly apparition opened its mouth to speak, the terrified waitress screamed, dropped the plates and fled from the building.

The room in which the female stranger died, number 8, is also apparently a favourite haunt of the ghost, who frequently appears there holding a candle. Indeed, while she was on her deathbed, the number 8 on the door is said to have turned sideways to form an "infinity" sign – and 200 years on, the female stranger shows no signs of leaving.

Rumours have abounded about her identity. She might, some say, have been Theodosia Burr, the vanished daughter of an unpopular politician, presumed dead but whispered by some to have run away with her lover. Others insist she was the aristocratic daughter of an English lord who eloped with – horror of horrors – a commoner. And still others believe she was Napoleon Bonaparte in disguise. The mysterious reason for her husband's insistence on anonymity, though, was truly taken to the grave – along with his unpaid bills.

BATTERSEA POLTERGEIST

The address 63 Wycliffe Road, Battersea, London doesn't exist anymore. The semi-detached Victorian house was demolished in the 1960s following a bizarre 12 years that left no one wanting to live there, because it appeared to have been haunted by a demented poltergeist.

The trouble started in 1956, when 15-year-old Shirley Hitchings, who lived there with her parents, grandmother and adopted brother, found an ornate silver key on her pillow. Her father Wally, a London Underground train driver, unsuccessfully tried the key in every lock in the house. That night the house was rocked by deafening thudding and banging noises that reminded the family of the Blitz, when London had been targeted by German bombers in the Second World War. The neighbours complained, but neither the police nor the surveyor who was brought in could locate the source of the noises that included eerie scratching inside the furniture, while lights flashed on and off during the night.

Over the following weeks the inexplicable racket got worse and the activity more extreme, several witnesses claiming to have seen slippers walking of their own accord, clocks floating through the air, pots and pans flung around the kitchen and chairs moving around the house. Shirley's screams woke the family one night when her sheets were wrenched from her bed and her body was pulled into the air.

Harold Chibbett, a ghost hunter, from then on devoted himself to the case, explaining the house was inhabited by a poltergeist – a German word meaning "noisy ghost". He said poltergeists were often attracted to teenaged girls. It was clear that this poltergeist – whom they named "Donald" after the bad-tempered Disney character Donald Duck – was obsessed with Shirley, the noises following her to work and causing her to lose not only her job as a seamstress, but also her friends, who believed she was possessed by the Devil.

National press coverage and even a mention in the House of Commons did nothing to calm the situation, and soon Wally had to give up work due to stress. Exorcisms were attempted, to no avail, but the family learned to communicate with Donald via alphabet cards and tapping.

Then Donald started replying in handwritten notes addressed to Shirley, the first of which read, "Shirley I come." Eventually, through notes, Donald identified himself as King Louis XVII of France, supposed to have died in captivity at the age of ten. Using elaborate French phrases, he claimed he had escaped, only to drown en route to England.

Donald's activities continued for years, with unexplained fires and voices. Scientific explanations have been proposed; could its location on unstable marshland have caused noises and movements, or the acidity of the soil resulted in madness? Shirley, who later wrote a book about the experience, also came under close scrutiny. Was Donald a figment of her teenage imagination, a means of drawing attention to herself and of swapping her sheltered existence for something more in line with her starry-eyed notions? Handwriting experts who analysed the huge number of messages she claimed to have received from Donald – as many as 60 a day – believed they were written by Shirley herself. Yet several people witnessed the extraordinary happenings, including the police.

With the poltergeist famous internationally, Shirley was able to move out of the house she had shared with her parents, and had money for clothes and more fashionable hairstyles. Donald was going quiet by the time Shirley married in 1965, and after she left London two years later, the poltergeist told her he was leaving.

Whatever the reality, Shirley stated that the prolonged episode robbed her of her childhood. In a 2021 interview, she said the haunting still feels as real as it was then. The house at number 63 is gone, but Donald has lived on in the minds of paranormal enthusiasts.

THE ROOM THAT WAS SPIRITED AWAY

The vast Banff Springs Hotel, first built in 1888 by the Canadian Pacific Railway, is situated amid pine-covered slopes and rivers in Banff National Park, high in the Rocky Mountains of Alberta province. The original building was wooden and burned down but was replaced in grand style over the following decades, its steep pitched roofs reminiscent of a French chateau. Natural hot spring water is piped in from nearby Sulphur Mountain for the enjoyment of the hotel's guests, who have included British royalty and celebrities such as Marilyn Monroe. But the iconic hotel is also said to have a number of more mysterious long-term guests.

The eighth storey once had a Room 873, but the door to that room was boarded over. Some say it's simply that the room was torn down to make a larger suite. But others say the room was closed off after guests were woken by hair-raising screams in the middle of the night, and bloody fingerprints would persistently appear on the walls or bathroom mirror. The gruesome story involves a family – a father, a mother and their little girl – who checked into Room 873 many years ago; the father went mad one night and slaughtered his wife and child in the room. Once the room was refurbished and put back into use, it seemed that the murdered mother and child had remained there in spirit.

Another ghostly apparition occasionally glimpsed in the historical building is that of "The Bride". Guests have reported seeing a woman in a white dress – sometimes appearing to be on fire – treading the marble staircase to the reception hall and then vanishing, leaving a cold chill in the air. In the ballroom, too, some claim to have seen a bride dancing alone at night, and heart-wrenching sobbing noises are sometimes heard coming from the empty bridal suite. The legend is that a young bride tragically met her end on her wedding day in the 1930s, after tripping on her bridal gown and falling down a staircase on her way to the ballroom. Some say she fell trying to put out the flames that were engulfing her dress after it caught fire as she brushed past the candles that were illuminating the staircase.

Thankfully, not all the stories are of untimely, tragic deaths. There's also said to be a friendly phantom at the hotel – the ghost of the old Scottish bellman, Sam McAuley, who worked there in the 1960s and into the 1970s, and refused to retire. He is thought to have died in 1976, but his spirit still seems to be working there to this day, usually on the ninth floor, where he helps unwitting guests with their bags, unlocks the door or turns on the room lights, vanishing if they try to talk to him or tip him.

Guests also still report other strange happenings: "something tugging on my dress" during dinner; a bedroom "turning cold"; and "something grabb[ing] my foot". The Banff Springs Hotel, now officially Fairmont Banff Springs, denies that it is haunted, but the lingering stories of its famous ghosts, together with its reputation for luxury and its proximity to the ski slopes, only seem to keep guests coming back for more.

GHOST CRASH

When several motorists called emergency services one night in December 2002 to report having seen the headlights of a car veer off the A3 – a main road between London and Portsmouth, England – and plummet down a grassy bank, the police went to investigate what they took to be a routine motor accident. However, on arriving at the scene, at the slip road to Burpham near Guildford, expecting to find an overturned vehicle in the ditch, they discovered no traces of anything untoward having happened there at all.

Puzzled by the fact that it wasn't just one passing motorist who claimed to have witnessed the crash, the police continued their search of the area, only to discover a car nose-down in a ditch a little further along the road, with enough rust to suggest it had been there for a while, and well hidden by the overgrown vegetation all around it. The battery of the car was flat. One further thing made them certain the accident had not only just occurred: close to the wrecked Vauxhall Astra lay a body that had clearly been lying there for some time.

After police identified him through the car's registration details, the remains were forensically confirmed as those of a 21-year-old man who was wanted for robbery and had been on the run. He had been reported missing by his family five months earlier, last seen drinking in Hounslow in south-west London, and from the decayed state of the wreckage, it seemed that the accident must have happened the night he went missing. The fact that his remains were found outside the car suggested that he had tried to clamber up the bank to get help but had been too badly injured.

All this led to local speculation that what the motorists had actually witnessed on that December night was a ghostly replay of the accident that had occurred five months previously, which would have remained unnoticed had those calls not been made about an accident that apparently hadn't happened.

Police dismissed the paranormal explanation, but the driver of the tow truck called out to remove the crashed vehicle remained haunted by his memory of it every time he drove past the spot.

A STRANGE GREEK GROTTO

Named after a notorious mid-nineteenth-century bandit who hid out in its maze of tunnels, Davelis Cave, 25 miles north of Athens, Greece, has a wealth of strange tales swirling around it, some going back more than 1,500 years, others much more recent. Stories of electronic gadgets malfunctioning, preternatural orbs glowing, ghostly voices calling out and a strange handprint only serve to bring more intrigued visitors to the vast grotto every year.

The cave – which averages 50 yards wide and 68 yards high – opens into the cliffs high on Mount Penteli. Two Byzantine chapels sit in the entrance, as well as a more recent military building, beyond which a series of tunnels lead to a pool, the whole thing part of an ancient quarry where the marble for buildings such as the Parthenon was dug. Devotees of Pan, the ancient Greek god of shepherds and orgies, among other things, and associated with various forms of mischief, used the cave as a shrine as far back as the fifth century, and hermits and monks flocked to what they called the "Cave of the Immaculate" in the Middle Ages, either for spiritual retreats or to escape persecution. It is rumoured that more recently, satanic rituals were held in its depths.

In the late 1970s, the cave's tunnels were classified as military and sealed off to the public, fuelling speculation. In 1982, a Greek author of paranormal and science fiction, Georgios Balanos, wrote *The Enigma of Penteli*, conjecturing about hidden tunnels and mind-control projects, while the media suggested it was the site of nuclear experiments. Suspicion was aroused when the Greek government abruptly sealed the cave off, claiming that they needed to dig new tunnels, but then ceased all excavating activity and abandoned the site.

Dimitrios Makridopoulos, a young computer technician, also claims secret military experiments were conducted in the cave in the 1970s and 1980s. In 2015, drawn there by his fascination with the occult, he visited with a "spirit box" and an infrared camera, which he hoped would allow him to communicate with, and record, supernatural presences.

"From the minute I stepped into this unspoilt and pure place... I was surrounded by an inexplicable, otherworldly energy," he said. "I felt eyes following my every move... I could not see or hear anything with my five senses, but I knew."

The spirit box, using radio frequencies, recorded an apparent choir of youthful angelic voices chanting in ancient Greek – a sound described by Makridopoulos as "the language of the pixies". And he also claimed that his camera picked up ghostly apparitions near the entrance.

Had the government's explanation about needing new tunnels been a cover-up to hide what was really going on – an investigation of paranormal activity in the cave?

Scientists claim that the graphite and the marble would make it a good conductor of electromagnetic waves, which might explain some of the strange feelings and phenomena experienced by many when walking within its depths.

While the truth has never emerged, to this day, there is no shortage of people willing to make the hike to the cave in a bid to experience its ethereal qualities themselves – and to wonder, as they enter, what went on there…

B&B WITH A SPIRIT OR THREE

Built in 1796 on an antebellum plantation in the small town of St Francisville near New Orleans, Louisiana, The Myrtles is today run as a successful bed and breakfast. Its success may be down to its attractive features – its colonial-style wrap-around veranda; its stained-glass front door etched into a cross to ward off evil; its French crystal chandelier hanging ostentatiously in its grand foyer.

Or possibly, it may be because of phantoms such as the "Ghost Girl", sometimes seen gazing through one of the windows, and its reputation as one of the most terrifying places to visit in America. Over the course of its long history, ten people are said to have been murdered in the mansion – and though there is no evidence for most of the stories, most of the unfortunates seem to still have an eerie presence there, with many reported sightings of ghosts.

The most famous is "Chloe", said to have been a slave on the plantation in the early 1800s. Wearing a green turban to hide the place where her ear was cut off for listening in to the owner's secret dealings, she is said to visit guests' rooms at night and stare at them. Some say Chloe baked a cake containing an extract of oleander leaves, which poisoned the owner's wife and daughters, and then was herself killed and thrown into the Mississippi River.

It was in the 1950s, when The Myrtles was sold to Marjorie Munson, that the ghost stories starting circulating, perhaps because Munson herself felt the house was haunted and so asked around. The property subsequently changed hands a couple of times, before being bought by James and Frances Kermeen Myers. Frances, who received death threats from the Ku Klux Klan and experienced the tragic loss of loved ones during her years there, has written about broken clocks starting to tick, beds floating up into the air, paintings flying across the room, locked doors suddenly shooting open, the crystal chandelier inexplicably shaking, hefty footsteps walking across the floor and ghostly piano music suddenly sounding in the dead of night.

Other spooky sightings include a young child seen bouncing on the beds, a voodoo priestess in the Old Nursery, and a previous owner, an attorney called William Winter, who lived there from 1865 until his death in 1871. Although popular in the plantation, he was shot in the chest by a stranger and died as he tried to climb the stairs. He expired on the seventeenth step, and visitors as well as staff have reported hearing his dying footsteps as he eternally staggers up the stairs.

All of this has led to The Myrtles being known as one of America's most haunted houses, where ghost tours are offered to anyone seeking a ghoulish thrill.

OLD CHANGI HOSPITAL: WARDING OFF LOST SOULS

Singapore's Old Changi Hospital was built by the British colonial government in 1935 and started out as a military medical facility. Two of its buildings were part of the Kitchener Barracks housing British Army soldiers from the Royal Engineers. During the Second World War, however, the hospital was taken over by the Japanese and although still used as a medical facility, its grounds also held prisoners of war.

After 1942, some of the hospital grounds were used by the Kempeitai, the Japanese military police force, which also served as secret police, and was known for ruthless torture methods and horrific executions. One room allegedly still has thick chains hanging from the walls and blood-stained floors – "allegedly" because the building is now cordoned off, with security officers making sure no one enters.

Following the surrender of the Japanese and the end of the war, the building went through a variety of guises before it became Changi Hospital, its services available to the general public. In 1997, the hospital was relocated, as the rickety old building proved inefficient. The building was now derelict, and that's when rack and ruin, and vandalism, set in – as well as, apparently, Satanists carrying out demonic rituals in some of the now abandoned rooms. A pentacle daubed in red paint on the floor of one of the rooms suggests the occurrence of occult practices there.

Spooky sightings have allegedly included apparitions in pre-war clothing and spirits dressed in medical uniforms. The ghosts of bloodied soldiers have been spotted wandering, as well as those of patients whose souls somehow never left the place. Those who died young are said to haunt the former children's ward, and loud, unexplained bangs, crashes and screams have been heard echoing down the corridors.

Given its spooky reputation, Changi attracts many curious about the ghostly presences. Sometimes a member of a group has vanished and then reappeared, claiming to have been lured into the corridors by a figure who seemed at first familiar but then warned them away, saying they should leave and not return.

There's definitely no hint of a gentle bedside manner in the Old Changi Hospital today...

ANCIENT RAM INN
SERVES SPIRITS

"The Ancient Ram Inn dates to Time Immemorial" states the wording on its deeds, written mostly in Norman French. Although the inn in the English county of Gloucestershire is said to have been constructed in 1145, it could certainly be even older.

Reportedly built on a Pagan burial site that may have dated back thousands of years, the inn first belonged to the church and then passed into private hands and was an inn and public house for centuries. It has typically crooked walls and creaky floorboards, and its dark, tortuous, oppressive passageways have seen enough grim times to account for the ghosts people claim to experience.

Legend has it that the troubled spirit of a sixteenth-century woman accused of being a witch haunts the room where she was hiding when she was captured and then burned at the stake. The ghost of a monk is said to make regular appearances in the first-floor "Bishop's Room", with guests often fleeing in terror in the middle of the night. A centurion on horseback reputedly startled a workman at the inn then disappeared through a wall. And as if all that wasn't enough, a supernatural seductress known as a succubus is reported to creep into the beds of sleeping guests from time to time...

Situated in the Cotswold village of Wotton-under-Edge, its location on two ley lines is believed by some to have endowed it with spiritual energy from Stonehenge, but the redirecting of water on the property is thought to have opened up a portal for dark energy to enter, causing the paranormal phenomena it is known for.

A previous owner of the place in the late 1960s, John Humphries, claimed that on his first night in the property, some force grabbed his arm and dragged him from his bed. Under the staircase, he discovered the skeletons of children with daggers lodged in their ribcages – remains that he took as evidence of ritual child sacrifice and devil worship, and that left him haunted by the entities he sensed in the house. Still, he remained living in the house along with the spirits right up until his death in 2017.

Other deceased former owners are reported to have been spotted sitting genially among living guests, most of whom are specifically there for the opportunity to rub shoulders with the dead. Today it is no longer a tavern, but Humphries' daughter keeps the inn open to some guests, and it functions mostly as the go-to place for anyone fancying a ghost hunt or spooky sleepover. One sceptical participant in a late-night ghost hunt there said she experienced enough unexplained events that she would never stay in the building alone.

MYSTIFYING LANDMARKS

Nature's most awe-inspiring wonders are often imbued with mystery. Take Uluru, named Ayers Rock by white settlers – the vast red rock in the middle of Australia. It's steeped in myth, legend and stories of the Dreamtime – the time of creation – and is the indigenous people's way of explaining this natural feature with its powerful aura.

For millennia, humans have also found ways of creating structures that evoke similar fascination. How did the ancient Anasazi cliff dwellers of what is now North America construct monumental buildings hundreds of feet up a sheer rock face? And, just as compellingly, why?

This chapter looks at these and other natural and man-made landmarks that have mystified people for centuries. How, without wheels or engines, and in extremely inhospitable conditions, did primitive people erect such complex structures as the Great Pyramids of Egypt or the statues on Easter Island?

There are often no definitive answers to these questions – educated guesses will have to suffice in many cases. Yet even where a definitive answer has been supplied, as in the case of the crop-circle phenomenon that confounded the world in the late 1970s, later exposed as a hoax, there seems to be a need to hold on to the mysterious element that captivated us – to believe that there's more to them than meets the eye.

The large crowds of people seen marvelling every day at Stonehenge, from a considerable distance, and surrounded by sheep, are evidence of our perpetual fascination with these ancient, mesmerizing landmarks.

THE GREAT PYRAMIDS OF EGYPT: "LOOK ON MY WORKS, YE MIGHTY"

Pyramids were built by the ancient Egyptians from 2600 BCE to 1550 BCE as elaborate tombs from which the dead person could begin their journey of transformation to the afterlife. The size and grandeur of these feats of architecture reflected the power and wealth of the pharaoh or high-ranking official lying inside. The Great Pyramid of Giza, one of the so-called Seven Wonders of the Ancient World, was constructed using over 2 million stone blocks of limestone and granite, each weighing more than 2 tons.

Over 100 pyramids have been identified, most of them grouped together here and there along the River Nile's west bank. But although extensive research has been carried out on the pyramids since the nineteenth century (including ill-advised early excavations), many unanswered questions remain about these massive structures.

How did the ancient Egyptians build them without any machinery, bringing blocks sometimes hundreds of miles? Wheels were mainly used for making pottery before 1500 BCE, and in any case wheeled carts would have struggled in thick sand. One theory put forward in 2014 originated from a detail in a painting from 1900 BCE, showing men pulling a statue on a sled while another stands pouring something on the sand ahead. A new interpretation of this suggested that dampening the sand would have made it firmer, perhaps allowing the heavy building blocks to be dragged across it.

How the blocks were lifted into place is another mystery. A ramp found in a quarry indicates that the ancient Egyptians were able to pull enormously heavy stone blocks up steep slopes, so it's possible that they employed a similar process for hauling them up the sides of the pyramids. Theories have been proposed suggesting wooden sleds, rollers or posts strapped around the block's sides to make it easier to manoeuvre up ramps that might have spiralled around the outside of the pyramid – yet the mind still boggles at the notion.

A further puzzle concerns what lies inside the vast cavities of the pyramids. Despite the cavalier excavating activity of early archaeologists, they were never intended to be opened and the Egyptian government has banned any further projects that would harm the structures, but modern non-invasive scanning techniques have been used on the Pyramid of Khufu, revealing voids of various sizes inside that could be passageways, galleries or chambers. Hailed as breakthrough discoveries by scientists, they could hold answers to some of the questions about the engineering techniques used in the pyramids' construction.

And why, finally, did the Egyptians stop building pyramids, with bodies thereafter being buried in underground tombs instead? It may have been due to changes in religious practices from 1500 BCE, when the last was created, or because of lack of space in the new capital of Luxor, the high cost of construction or persistent plundering. Alternatively, it could have been a realization that – although we now see these structures as some of the most indestructible ever designed – the extreme hot and cold temperatures of the desert, which would have caused the stone to expand and contract, were leading to cracking and the gradual disintegration of the pyramids' outer casing. As a result, the pyramids were becoming sad ruins rather than lasting symbols of perfection. The Romantic poet Percy Bysshe Shelley wrote in "Ozymandias", inspired by the statue of the Sphinx lying near the Great Pyramid:

> My name is Ozymandias, King of Kings;
> Look on my Works, ye Mighty, and despair!
> Nothing beside remains. Round the decay
> Of that colossal Wreck, boundless and bare
> The lone and level sands stretch far away.

ROLLRIGHT STONES

Brine shrimp were the unlikely participants in an experiment aimed at solving the mystery of an ancient circle of stones in a rural field in the English county of Oxfordshire.

The Rollright Stones are natural boulders of Jurassic oolitic limestone found locally and include a solitary tall stone, a large circle of more than 70 smaller stones of different shapes and sizes, and an outlying cluster. They are traditionally said to be a king and his men who were turned to stone by a witch. Despite the allure of the legend of the petrified royal party, the whole group could well have been part of a 5,000-year-old burial chamber or dolmen, perhaps used ceremonially. Though little can be known for certain, many theories have been put forward over the years surrounding the phenomenon of such standing stones, or megaliths.

Many have claimed that sites such as this are gathering and distribution hubs for the Earth's energy, distributed in invisible track lines as electromagnetic radiation. Powerful reactions have been recorded to dowsing, a recognized system for detecting earth energies by using twigs, a rod or a pendulum. Some have also found that the energy charge at such sites can be affected by the moon. Investigating a large standing stone in Wales in 1975, physicist Eduardo Balanovski discovered significant magnetic anomalies and suggested "the people who put it there knew about its power, even if they didn't know about electromagnetism". The energy could be linked to the concept of ley lines, ancient pilgrimage routes or spirit paths between sacred sites.

As mystical as the "earth-energy" explanation appears to some, it has certainly garnered support from numerous scientific researchers, and among them was a biologist who used a fishy means of demonstrating that there are indeed magnetic fields at work around the Rollright Stones. When Harry Oldfield placed a blacked-out jar of shrimp near each stone in August 1981, the shrimp, which are known to be highly sensitive to magnetic fields, all moved in a cluster towards the stones.

The Dragon Project, which had monitored the Rollright Stones over a protracted period beginning in the late 1970s, likewise included scientists on its team – among them physicists, electronics engineers and an inorganic chemist – and made use of modern equipment such as hand-held ultrasonic detectors and Geiger counters from the late 1970s. They were certainly primed for startling results, with team member Paul Devereux recounting the following anecdote:

On one occasion a Dragon Project monitor, working in the misty pre-dawn hours at the King Stone, got the fright of his life when he saw shadowy figures passing near the monolith. Summoning up his courage, he approached the beings to find they were in fact soldiers on a training exercise making for the Royal Observer Corps bunker in the King Stone field!

Some radioactive anomalies were indeed picked up, but their findings, though tantalizing, were inconclusive. If the Rollright

Stones and other standing stones do indeed possess the power that many are convinced they do, another question remains to be answered: were these megaliths built at certain locations because those places were already known to possess power, or did the circles gain their power through centuries – or even millennia – of spiritual use? With their origins so long ago, that part of the mystery will perhaps remain unsolved forever.

MACHU PICCHU: SACRED CITADEL

Known as the "Lost City of the Incas", the fifteenth-century citadel of Machu Picchu (probably meaning "old mountain" or "old peak") was built so high up in the Andes, above the clouds, that it remained hidden from the rest of the world – and thus very well preserved – until 1911.

Machu Picchu is the most visited tourist destination in Peru, and is famous for its intricate dry-stone-wall construction and its more than 100 separate flights of stairs, most carved from one slab of stone. But because the Inca civilization had no written language, no record was left explaining how the site was built (many believe no wheels were used, and hundreds of men would have pushed each of the massive slabs up the mountain), why it was built, or why it was mysteriously abandoned only a century after it was built.

Modern archaeologists have made use of the surviving physical evidence, including tombs, to reconstruct what its more than 150 buildings might have been used for – they appear to range from baths and houses to temples and sanctuaries – as well as to determine who the inhabitants might have been, and why they left so soon. By 1976, a third of Machu Picchu had been restored, and the work had been ongoing until 2023, when the site was shut down indefinitely due to political unrest in Peru.

The citadel is generally thought to have been built in around 1450 as a country estate for the Inca emperor Pachacuti, probably after a successful military campaign, and abandoned during the Spanish conquest a century later. Around 750 people lived and worked there, most of whom may have died of smallpox brought into the community by travellers before the Spanish conquistadors arrived there.

An alternative theory suggests that Machu Picchu was built by the sun-worshipping Incas to serve as an astronomical observatory. The citadel and all of its buildings are in alignment with spiritually significant mountains framing the sunrises and sunsets during the equinoxes and solstices, which were important events in the Inca calendar. Its sacred Intihuatana stone also indicates the two equinoxes, when the sun sits directly over the stone, creating no shadow.

The fact that Machu Picchu lies high above the Sacred Valley, on a mountain ridge 2,660 yards above sea level, has led to another theory that it was built as the final stop on a challenging pilgrimage starting out in Cuzco, an even higher city in south-eastern Peru, with an elevation of 3,720 yards.

Regardless of its true purpose, which may never be definitively known, Machu Picchu is an archaeological treasure, and in recognition of this, in 2007 it was voted one of the "New Seven Wonders of the World" in a worldwide internet poll.

GLASTONBURY TOR: RISING FROM THE MIST

Just outside the small town of Glastonbury in the English county of Somerset, and visible for many miles around, is Glastonbury Tor, a hill imbued with so much spiritual and magical symbolism that people are drawn to it from all over the world.

In a roughly conical shape yet stepped with deep terraces, the Tor is an age-old site, where Neolithic flint tools have been found, along with evidence of an Iron Age settlement, pre-Christian burials, Roman pottery and the remains of medieval burials. On top stands the tall, roofless St Michael's Tower, all that is left of a church that was demolished during the sixteenth-century Dissolution of the Monasteries. While the tower is the point many people head for when they climb the Tor, the hill itself is the focus of many legends that purport to explain the importance of the site.

A Christian legend says that Joseph of Arimathea established the first Church of England at Glastonbury and brought Jesus himself to the Tor. It's certainly feasible that there was a very early Christian church there, and some claim that the Holy Grail was buried in the town. A twelfth-century historian mentioned that the coffins of King Arthur and Queen Guinevere were found here and later moved. Medieval monks named Glastonbury Tor as the gateway to Avalon (meaning "Land of the Dead").

Glastonbury Tor rises abruptly 173 yards above the flat land of the Somerset Levels, which is often shrouded in early-morning mist. The hill's Celtic name was Ynys Wydryn or Ynys Gutrin, meaning "Isle of Glass". Thousands of years ago, the area around it would have been a sea, and later a lake; and even today it often appears to rise out of the thick, cold mist floating like a white sea around it. A scientific explanation for this visual illusion is that rays of light bend as they pass through layers of air of varying temperatures, producing what is known as a "Fata Morgana" – a term which itself refers back to Arthurian legend, Morgan le Fay being the name of Arthur's sorceress sister.

The sides of the Tor contain a particularly mysterious feature: seven deep, roughly symmetrical terraces that some historians suggest are the remains of a "spiral walkway", or labyrinth, created for pilgrims to reach the church of St Michael at the summit after circling the Tor seven times. According to Welsh mythology, however, the terraces are a maze leading to the entrance to Annwn, the Otherworld.

A more down-to-earth explanation for the terraces is that they were constructed during the Middle Ages to make ploughing easier, yet the terracing continues round the north side, where crops wouldn't have been able to grow. The earthworks might, alternatively, have been built as defensive ramparts, possibly linked to Ponter's Ball Dyke nearby.

In the town nestled beneath the Tor lie the spectacular ruins of Glastonbury Abbey, itself significant for being the point at which the powerful Michael and Mary ley lines are said to intersect, amplifying universal and earth energy, and providing another reason for the constant stream of truth-seekers to the area.

NAZCA LINES

A complex and unique series of patterns in the Nazca Desert, high up in the Peruvian Andes, has confounded explanation so much that aliens have been invoked to explain their puzzling presence.

Presumed to date from around 2,000 years ago, and perhaps created over several hundred years, many are simple lines and geometric shapes and appear to have been drawn by removing a layer of rocks to expose paler dirt beneath. In the early part of the present century, Joe Nickell, an American investigator of the paranormal, religious artefacts and folk mysteries, replicated this method of creating the lines using tools and technology that would have been available to the Nazca people.

But what makes them extraordinary is that quite a few, depicting animals and plants – from a hummingbird to a monkey – are so huge that they are indistinguishable on the ground, and can only be fully appreciated by looking down on them from the sky – though visible from high places. For this reason, their presence was only noted in detail when Peruvian pilots reported them in the early twentieth century. The ancient Nazca people had no known means of flying, so why go to such great effort to make them?

Archaeologists, historians and mathematicians have come up with a wide range of theories, including that the Nazca people wanted them to be seen by deities. Other researchers, such as Paul Kosok and Maria Reiche, proposed that the lines were intended as a kind of astronomical observatory, indicating where the sun and other celestial bodies rose or set during the solstices, as Stonehenge is said to do. Still others have suggested that the lines had a variety of agricultural, social and astronomical functions. But none of this explains how the Nazca would have mapped out such vast shapes.

Perhaps the most famous theory of all was put forward by the Swiss author Erich von Däniken, a strong believer in earthly visitations by extraterrestrials. In his best-selling 1968 book *Chariots of the Gods?*, he proposed that the mysterious Nazca shapes and lines resembled those of modern airport runways, and that they therefore represented landing sites for UFOs. He related an ancient Sanskrit story in which "human-like beings with golden, shimmering skins" disembarked from an alien spacecraft, mined for metals and then flew away. These other-worldly astronauts were said to have soon returned to build some of the Nazca landing tracks, and then to have left again – prompting the native people to continue their work, regarding them as gods and hoping the lines would encourage them to return. But they never did.

Although scientists and archaeologists dismissed von Däniken's ideas as absurd and considered his work to be without intellectual credibility or literary merit, his books have nevertheless attracted thousands of visitors to the Nazca Lines, many of them continuing to be firm believers in the "alien runway" theory, and perhaps hoping that one day the mysterious visitors will return.

CHAUVET CAVE PAINTINGS

The discovery in 1994 of a series of remarkable paintings in a cave in Chauvet-Pont d'Arc, south-east France, presented a number of puzzling questions.

When they were first unearthed by three scientists, it was thought that the sophisticated and well-preserved drawings – over 1,000 of them, including bears, lions, rhinoceros and even woolly mammoth, and on the move rather than static – were so advanced that they were probably between 12,000 and 17,000 years old.

But later research using new geomorphological and chlorine-36 dating techniques showed that the paintings had to have been completed before a series of rockslides sealed the cave entrance 21,000 years ago. As a result, French scientists now believe that they were created by early humans around 36,000 years ago, making them, according to one academic journal, "the oldest and most elaborate [cave paintings] ever discovered".

Still, another mystery remained: what were the intriguing red and white splodges found in a spray shape alongside the depictions of animals on the limestone wall meant to be? The general opinion was that they were simply abstract designs – until a geological survey in the Ardèche region, where the cave is located, revealed that a volcanic eruption occurred there at around the same time as the paintings were created.

"It is very likely that humans living in the Ardèche river area witnessed one or several eruptions," explained one of the scientists, Jean-Michel Geneste. "We propose that the spray-shape signs found in the Chauvet-Pont d'Arc cave could be the oldest known depiction of a volcanic eruption."

Previously, paintings found in the 1960s at the Çatalhöyük settlement in Turkey depicting a volcanic eruption that happened 8,900 years ago had been thought to be the world's oldest. The cave paintings at Chauvet undoubtedly give an enigmatic glimpse into a shadowy era of human existence.

ULURU: THE "GREAT PEBBLE"

In 2019, a healthy 64-year-old man attempted to climb the sacred rock of Uluru, which rises more than 410 yards above the desert in the remote heart of the Australian outback. Three quarters of the way up, he had a heart attack. Luckily for him, two off-duty police officers and two paramedics were on his tour group and performed life-saving CPR on him before he was airlifted to hospital in Alice Springs, the closest settlement, 280 miles away.

European settlers called the massive 550-million-year-old single stone Ayers Rock, but to the Anangu, its traditional indigenous owners, it has been known as Uluru ("Great Pebble") since before the Ice Age. The fascinating shape and colour of what scientists call an inselberg, or "island mountain", has proved a lure to many climbers, but in the early 1990s, signs were erected saying "Please Don't Climb", as the Anangu regard the activity as sacrilegious. In their tradition, that was the route taken by ancestral men when they arrived at the sacred rock during the Dreamtime – the very beginning of time, when ancestral spirits breathed life into the environment and all its life forms. They believe that misfortune will befall anyone who attempts to scale the rock.

At least 30 people who have ignored the warning signs placed around its base and climbed it anyway have died before ever reaching the top. Were those 30 cases just plain bad luck, or should they have heeded the warnings of the Anangu, whose ancestors have lived there for 30,000 years?

Taking pieces of the rock away is equally frowned upon, and some holidaymakers, believing that they have been dogged by bad luck ever since making their ill-considered choice of souvenir, have resorted to mailing the stolen chunks back.

The ever-changing colour of the ancient rock that is steeped in myth, legend and mystery is part of its mystique, ranging from bright pink in the morning to orange at noon to silver-grey and black during the rare wet periods that only the Anangu seem able to predict.

Uluru's mysterious power and energy are thought by some to come from its location on the same major planetary grid point as the Great Pyramid in Egypt and the Bermuda Triangle. According to Aboriginal legend, the rock is situated at the crossroads between all of the sacred paths that run through Central Australia. Still others believe Uluru is a mythical animal with magical powers.

Climbing Uluru was officially banned in 2019, and one thing is certain: it's unwise ever to get into a battle of wills with the great red rock of Australia.

CASTEL DEL MONTE: FOLLY OR FORTRESS?

In a remote part of Italy, an enigmatic, octagonal thirteenth-century castle stands alone on a hilltop, surrounded by tall, pale turrets but with no moat or drawbridge or any obvious military function. The odd design of the grand Castel del Monte ("Castle of the Mountain"), located in the Puglia region in the south-east of the country with no settlement or port to protect, includes arrow slits set so deep that they would have been useless for firing arrows through.

And yet Castel del Monte was built by one of the most learned and cultured figures in Italian history, Frederick II, Holy Roman Emperor and King of Sicily. In addition to Castel del Monte – the grandest and strangest of his structures – Frederick built a string of much more functional castles and coastal fortresses across Puglia.

Castel del Monte has eight corner towers and eight rooms on each floor, one room leading into the next, and eight windows on the lower floor, leading to speculation about the significance of the number eight (with its connections to infinity). One theory is that the octagon is symbolic of the intersection of earth (square) and sky (circle). Others say the shape was inspired by the Dome of the Rock in Jerusalem, which Frederick would have seen while on the Sixth Crusade. Some have connected the striking construction with the Knights Templar, and Umberto Eco based an old fortress in *The Name of the Rose* on it.

So why did Frederick build Castel del Monte? The castle's dominant position, making it visible from afar, gives a clue, as well as the original ornateness of the interior and the fact that in its design it resembles a crown. For that, in effect, was its function – to act as a symbol of Frederick's lofty status and great power.

In fact, the oddly magnificent structure even enabled Frederick to continue to wield his power after his death, when it was used to imprison his unfortunate heirs. In later years, however, it was simply allowed to crumble to a ruin. When it was acquired by the Italian state in 1876 and turned into a national monument, it was in a poor condition and its stonework and marble features required extensive restoration.

Despite appearing to have been built as little more than a folly, the castle features today on Italy's currency. But perhaps what says most about the fleeting nature of status and power is the fact that the coin it appears on is worth nothing more than a single cent.

SECRETS OF STONEHENGE

Stonehenge, the megalithic circle on Salisbury Plain in the south of England, is not only one of the most iconic archaeological sites in the world, it's also one of the most mysterious. The standing sarsen stones of the outer ring rise around 8 yards in the air, each weighing upwards of 20 tons, some with lintels. Clearly, it was the work of the Arthurian wizard Merlin – who else could have transported the massive stones from Ireland, where they had been assembled by giants? Or was it the Danes, or the Romans?

Almost 5,000 years after it was built, most probably by ancient Britons, who left no written record as to how or why they erected the monument, intense debate continues to rage over both questions.

Archaeological investigation has been going on at Stonehenge since the seventeenth century and pieces of the puzzle are added from time to time. Research has revealed that it took more than 1,000 years and well over 20 million hours to construct. The jury is still out as to whether the bluestones (the smaller stones in the structure) were floated, dragged and hauled 145 miles from West Wales or were brought there much earlier by ice-age glaciers. The 30 sarsen stones forming the outermost ring are known to have been added later, around 2,500 BCE. In 2020, a core sample from them, taken in 1958, was returned and, thanks to the latest science, proved that they came from some 15 miles away, near Marlborough.

Yet despite the solving of certain questions, debate continues as to the monument's meaning or use. It's been linked by some to Druid worship, while others have claimed that it's a landing strip for alien spacecraft, and still others say it's a giant fertility symbol.

The site's alignment to the sun and moon points to its use for rituals linked to the changing seasons and the summer and winter solstices, and its alignment with certain stars indicates its use as a megalithic calendar for working out dates and predicting astronomical events such as solar eclipses. Was it a giant solar calendar with links to ancient Egypt?

Meanwhile, research linking various prehistoric sites across Britain has begun to form a picture of possible ceremonial or sacred routes forming a network between them. The Preseli Hills of Wales are dotted with ancient tombs or dolmens, along with ancient quarries, which could have been the source of the Stonehenge bluestones.

A new theory has recently emerged based on the magical powers associated with the bluestones – namely, that it was a site people came to for healing. Bronze Age skeletons with bone deformities have been unearthed around the site.

The mystery surrounding Stonehenge continues to fuel the popularity of the stones, rated as Europe's best-known prehistoric monument. Access to the inner circle is now only possible early in the morning or late in the evening, by reservation.

Vincent Gaffney, UK lead for the Stonehenge Hidden Landscapes Project, was quoted by the BBC as saying, "It frequently seems that there is always something new from Stonehenge, but I continue to be surprised that we keep finding so much – even in areas that have been studied intensively for years."

THE GEORGIA GUIDESTONES

Although it was sometimes called the "Stonehenge of America", a set of granite stones, erected in 1980 by a mysterious benefactor, did not have anywhere near the same longevity as the 5,000-year-old English landmark. The stones took a year to build and a mere 42 years after they suddenly appeared in a field in the US state of Georgia, they were destroyed.

The identity of the man who ordered their construction, claiming to represent "a small group of loyal Americans", has never become public knowledge. To this day, he is known only by the pseudonym Robert C. Christian.

Despite the anonymity surrounding this group, it had a clear mission and message: its members believed the world was heading for a global calamity, and they wanted the monument to serve as a guide for whoever survived.

And they knew exactly where they wanted their message to be broadcast from: Elberton, Georgia. The small rural town was known as the "Granite Capital of the World", growing up alongside a massive 35-mile-long deposit of the hard rock that most of its buildings, signs and gravestones are made from.

Until 1980, there was nothing else particularly remarkable about Elberton. On 22 March of that year, however, in a humble cow field north of the town, a 119-ton monument was unveiled to 400 invited onlookers: four 19-foot-tall slabs of blue granite arranged in an X around a central column, with a capstone. It had been built by a local firm, who agreed to keep the identity of Robert C. Christian a secret.

Sandblasted into the stones were ten "commandments" in several languages, including Arabic, Chinese, Russian and Swahili – as well as English – stressing the importance of honouring the environment, keeping the world population below 500 million, and creating a global language. The location is close to what Cherokee Indians call "the centre of the world", with views east and west.

The stones became a popular tourist destination, as well as acting as a sundial, attracting many visitors during the 2017 solar eclipse. However, their messages stirred up controversy in the southern state and the stones were subjected to vandalism. Conspiracy theorists accused them of promoting eugenics, and locals claimed the site was being used at night by occult groups. Through social media, these accusations only grew more persistent, and in July 2022, Kandiss Taylor, a candidate in the election for state governor, promised to destroy the stones if she was elected, and tweeted that God "can do ANYTHING... That includes striking down Satanic Guidestones." Shortly after, one of the stones was blown up in the early hours of the morning, in what was described as an act of "domestic terrorism".

The remaining stones were then considered unsafe and were taken down. Although this didn't put an end to the controversy, there was also an overwhelming reaction of sadness from those who'd come to view the 42-year-old monument as part of their heritage. Among the latter were many of the local university students who had enjoyed gathering at the monument in the evenings, as well as the craftsmen responsible for building the modern henge.

Today, the surviving granite slabs are kept in storage, and all that remains in the cow field is a small circle of rubble – an ironic end for a monument bearing the message: "Be not a cancer on the earth. Leave room for nature."

GÖBEKLI TEPE: THE POTBELLIED HILL

The discovery of the oldest man-made place of worship in the world on Göbekli Tepe ("Potbelly Hill") in Turkey's south-eastern province of Urfa not only presented archaeologists with many fresh mysteries, but proved how little we really know about how humans lived before records began and what knowledge they had.

The ruins were found in the 1960s but their significance – the extent of the site and their age – didn't begin to be understood for several decades. Dating back perhaps as far as 10,000 BCE, and consisting of circular structures supported by the world's oldest megaliths, many decorated with intricately carved wild animals, it was constructed long before archaeologists believed any temples existed, 6,000 years before Stonehenge.

It was thought that after the Ice Age, food was too scarce for anything but a nomadic lifestyle, and that people in this area, known as Upper Mesopotamia, would perhaps have hunted gazelles. The hunter-gatherers who built Göbekli had no written language, no metal for tools, no pottery artefacts, and no domesticated animals or plants, and agriculture was at least 500 years in the future. So why would they choose to build a permanent place of worship?

The first archaeologist to excavate the site in the 1990s, Klaus Schmidt, was convinced the unique ancient buildings could turn current thinking on its head, however, changing our ideas about when and why humans started farming, and when they began living in permanent settlements and started practising organized religion.

The construction of the site raises much the same questions as that of the Pyramids and Stonehenge. A huge number of prehistoric flint tools such as knives and axes have been found scattered over the hill, providing the answer as to how the hunter-gatherers had cut and carved the massive 10-ton, 16-feet-tall stone pillars. However, then they had to haul them across the hill and arrange them in the ritualistic circular pattern they remain in today.

One reason the site was so well preserved is that many of the temple sites seem to have been mysteriously filled with earth before the site was abandoned. Radar and geomagnetic surveys have detected at least 16 further megalithic circles underground, providing yet more unanswered questions and the predicted need for another 50 years of excavations of the ancient site to find out more about the people who built it, and what happened to them.

SUBMERGED WONDERS OF ALEXANDRIA: TWENTY THOUSAND OBJECTS UNDER THE SEA

Looking out across the Mediterranean from Alexandria, Egypt's second-largest city, there's nothing to betray the fact that 5 yards beneath the waters lies a treasure trove that may hold the key to one of the abiding mysteries of the region's ancient civilization.

It was in 1996 that the submerged island of Antirhodos was discovered beneath the city's eastern harbour by a team of underwater archaeologists, led by Franck Goddio. The island is thought to have sunk following a massive earthquake centred on Crete that shook the entire Mediterranean region in 365 CE, followed by a deadly tsunami that killed thousands of people. A Roman soldier at the time described a terrible tremor followed by the sea receding far away, only to roar back with terrifying power.

As the team of divers descended, what they discovered was breathtaking: more than 20,000 objects were found scattered over the seabed, including colossal, perfectly intact Egyptian statues and sphinxes; a temple to Caesar; a temple to Isis, the Egyptian goddess of healing and magic; Mark Antony's unfinished palace, the Timonium; as well as columned avenues, monuments, a port, and the wreck of a 2,000-year-old Roman ship.

But the jewel in the crown was a royal residence believed to have been the palace of Cleopatra, the last pharaoh of Egypt, who died in 30 BCE, but whose final resting place with her lover Mark Antony has never been discovered. The palace may have been abandoned soon after Cleopatra's death, when Egypt was absorbed into the Roman Republic, and it's possible that the palace of Antirhodos is where Cleopatra chose to be buried.

Only further archaeological exploration of this site and the other possible locations of the tomb in the region around Alexandria will provide the long-awaited answer. For now, a Bust of Cleopatra believed to have come from Antirhodos is displayed in the Royal Ontario Museum, Canada, purchased in the early twentieth century by the museum's founder.

CROP CIRCLES: SERIOUS ABOUT CEREOLOGY

In the late 1970s, a phenomenon emerged that not only put the UK at the centre of a unique form of UFO hysteria, but also led to the creation of a whole new field of scientific enquiry: cereology.

Overnight, mysterious intricate patterns appeared in the wheat fields of the south of England – whirls and sharp angles radiating off circles, sometimes within bigger circles, the whole often resembling a huge bicycle-gear mechanism. Those who saw them – not just members of the public, but also scientists and academics – were baffled. As with phenomena such as the Nazca Lines of Peru, they could only be truly appreciated when seen from above.

Standing in a wheat field in Kent gazing upon a large area where the crops had been flattened into a remarkable pattern of otherworldly shapes, a retired engineer exclaimed, "No human could have done this."

Speculation linked the crop circles to alien visitors with superior intelligence, the shapes resembling landing spots for "flying saucers"; others posited ancient spiritual forces, weather anomalies picking up electrically charged matter, or secret weapons tests. Books were written on the subject and became bestsellers, and the Independent Crop Circle Researchers' Association was founded in the US. In the UK alone, at least 35 people claimed to be expert cereologists.

Crop circles then began to spring up in other parts of the world. Some were patently "fake", their creators motivated by art. But people continued to insist on the paranormal origins of others. Some cereologists began to seek government funding to assist them in their quest for answers. It was then that two men from Southampton decided that enough was enough and confessed that the whole thing was a hoax, and that they had been behind it.

In September 1991, Doug Bower and Dave Chorley admitted to a British newspaper reporter that they had dreamed up the idea in a pub one evening in 1978, "wondering what we could do for a bit of a laugh". Using nothing more sophisticated than a 4-foot-long wooden plank, a ball of string and a baseball cap with wire threaded through the visor to act as a sighting device, they had spent the next 13 years creating up to 30 new circles each growing season, always under the cover of night. Their efforts had clearly inspired others elsewhere.

Some of those who had been excited by the mystery or potential contact with beings from another planet were disappointed to have been conned. But the confession wasn't enough to deflate the die-hard circle enthusiasts, some of whom continue to believe that even if they are all man-made, their creation must have "been prompted by an independent nonhuman mind".

As for the retired engineer, his passion for crop circles remains. "The two gents may have hoaxed some of the circles," he said, "but the phenomenon is still there, and we will carry on research."

HIGH AND DRY IN THE DESERT

Mystery surrounds the Anasazi people who, for 1,000 years, lived in remarkable cliff settlements built some 600 feet high in the rocky canyons of the American Southwest, surrounded by desert. It was a great Neolithic civilization, creating elaborately decorated pottery, colourful loom-woven textiles and intricate rock art.

Then suddenly, within the space of 25 years, between 1275 and 1300 CE, all building work ceased, and the Anasazi upped sticks and moved out, leaving us to wonder not only how they had built those lofty homes, so well protected and easily defended in the cliffs, but what went so catastrophically wrong for them to suddenly and permanently vacate them.

It's believed that the fearless Anasazi builders clambered up the sheer cliff faces on ladders made of notched tree trunks propped hundreds of feet off the ground; indeed, some of the ladders are still in place today. Yet some ruins would not have been reachable by ladder, and how they were constructed remains intriguing. The buildings inside the cliffs were made of hand-cut stone blocks mortared together with clay-based adobe. Some structures are perched on rock ledges and tucked into cracks.

Others are massive, with ceilings weighing as much as 90 tons. The houses were then plastered and painted. All have survived in pristine condition because of the dry desert climate.

But why, having risked life and limb to build their rock metropolis, and indeed to learn to live in it, did the Anasazi then abandon it so completely? According to University of Colorado archaeologist Stephen Lekson, "After about 1200 CE, something very unpleasant happens."

Water is thought to have been a key factor, first in the flourishing of the cliff-dwelling Anasazi kingdom, but also in its downfall. Reliable rainfall kept the water tables topped up, enabling the settlements to thrive. But when the population had reached its highest level and was in need of a consistent supply of water, a severe drought hit, leading to malnutrition – with some groups possibly resorting to cannibalism to avoid starvation – as well as warfare, mass slaughter and destruction.

The migration to more luxuriant places further south, however, seems to have been abrupt. Ladles were left in bowls and granaries were abandoned with sacks full of grain inside – as though their intention was to return. But they never did, perhaps being drawn instead to the Kachina Cult of the Pueblo people, who had hundreds of deities interceding with the gods to ensure rain and fertility.

The non-cliff-dwelling descendants of the Anasazi include the modern Tewa, Acoma, Zuni and Hopi tribes. The magnificent cliff dwellings themselves remain empty, an ongoing source of fascination for succeeding generations.

THE EASTER ISLAND GIANTS

Easter Island is a tiny dot in the South Pacific Ocean, with its closest neighbour, Pitcairn Island, situated more than 1,240 miles distant, and Chile, the nearest mainland country, six hours away by air. Yet despite being one of the most remote inhabited places on the globe, a mere 64 square miles formed from volcanic eruptions, it is one of the most famous, because scattered across its surface are over 1,000 statues, averaging 13 feet high and weighing over 10 tons, carved from tuff, a compacted volcanic ash.

DNA testing on skeletons has shown that the Rapa Nui came from Polynesia around 1000 CE, and survived for centuries by farming sugar cane, bananas, taro and chickens, developing advanced social, political and religious systems. Dutch explorers gave the island its current name when they landed there on Easter Sunday in 1722.

Between around 1300 and 1600, in a very secretive process (according to an archaeologist dedicated to the project), master craftsmen carved nearly 2,000 giant stone figures, or moai. Around half never left the quarry site where they were sculpted – Rano Raraku, an extinct volcano. But close to 900 were transported to various sites around the island. The largest unfinished one, named "El Gigante", would have been 69 feet high – two thirds the height of the legendary Colossus of Rhodes, or the totem poles of the Haida peoples – and would have weighed an enormous 200 tons. Similar, though smaller, statues have been found in other parts of Polynesia.

Naturally, with no evidence remaining, people have puzzled over how these huge, heavy statues were moved. Although ropes, log rollers, wooden sleds and a vast amount of manpower were most likely involved, no attempts to replicate the process using the resources and technology that would have been available at the time have so far been successful.

The other question, of course, is what all those statues meant. It's believed that they were perhaps made to contain the spirits of their ancestors. Some of the statues are crowned by a red stone topknot, thought to confer power and status, and many are arranged around the perimeter of the island, facing inland. The Rapa Nui believed that their chiefs had come from the gods and would become divine once again after death, and it's possible that the moai of chiefs were placed there to watch over the islanders. Similar ancestor statues were also used as guardians on South Korea's volcanic Jeju Island from the mid-1700s, perhaps introduced by visitors from the sea.

Arguably the most mysterious of the statues, however, were buried up to their heads in a hillside. Was this to protect them?

Strangely, although the moai were carved with great care, many toppled over, probably a deliberate act by the islanders themselves in the eighteenth century, when a lack of food and fuel led to civil war. Further destruction followed in the nineteenth century, when the Rapa Nui were all but wiped out by the slave trade and by Christian missionaries' impact on their identity and culture. The native population rebounded, however, and still considers the moai sacred. And the rest of the world continues to be fascinated by the mysteries of Easter Island.

SUSPICIOUS DEATHS

The end of a person's life can be natural and peaceful – or it can be shockingly sudden and shrouded in mystery.

This chapter looks at cases where the Grim Reaper came calling out of the blue – or at least that's how it may look to those who discover the body – and the questions of how, who and why that can make them heart-wrenching, disturbing or fascinating. Especially when, despite years of minutely detailed investigations, answers remain uncertain.

A group of experienced hikers meet gruesome deaths when they all inexplicably abandon their tent one freezing night; a disgraced flamboyant millionaire is found floating naked in the sea 15 miles from his luxury yacht; a woman is found murdered in her own home, but it seems impossible for her husband, the only suspect, to have done it...

When someone comes to an untimely end in mysterious circumstances, whether they're a world-famous celebrity like Princess Diana or an unknown recluse, there's an overwhelming need to know what happened – what went so tragically wrong. We scour the newspapers and search online to find out what happened – perhaps in a "there but for the grace of God" frame of mind. Because if it could happen to them, could we be next?

THE IMPOSSIBLE MURDER

On the evening of 20 January 1931, in the northern English city of Liverpool, Julia Wallace was found by her husband of 16 years in their living room, bludgeoned to death.

Suspicion immediately settled on the husband, 52-year-old William Wallace, an insurance salesman, even though he had an apparently watertight alibi: the previous evening while at the chess club, he had been handed a message telling him to go to 25 Menlove Gardens East at 7.30 p.m. the following evening to discuss an insurance policy with an "R. M. Qualtrough". When the time came, he had indeed left the house, Julia had bolted the gate behind him and he had boarded the tram.

When he tried to find the address, however, he discovered – after asking numerous people in the area, including a policeman and a newsagent (perhaps he wanted them to remember him?) – that "Menlove Gardens East" didn't exist. About 45 minutes later, he returned home. But on arriving there, he told his neighbours, who were heading out for the evening, that he appeared to have been locked out. When he tried the back door again, while they watched, it opened. Inside, he made the gruesome discovery of his wife's battered body, and rushed out again saying, "Oh, come and see, she's been killed."

The police soon arrived, and the forensics expert determined the time of death – by the extent to which rigor mortis had set in – to have been around 8 p.m., when Wallace had proof that he had been on the other side of the city.

Even though a milk delivery boy claimed to have seen Julia alive around the time her husband had set off, the police decided that if Wallace had been quick, he would still have had enough time to have committed the murder and got across the city. But given the brutal nature of the killing, what of the blood? No significant trace of blood was found; the bath and drains were examined and had not been recently used, though a coat was found underneath Julia's body, which could have been used to shield the killer from the blood.

Wallace was arrested, and at his trial the jury agreed with the police, even though the evidence was entirely circumstantial. He was convicted of murder and sentenced to hang. Throughout the proceedings Wallace claimed he was innocent, and the Court of Criminal Appeal eventually overturned the jury's verdict, saying it was "not supported by the weight of the evidence".

Presumably it would have been possible for Wallace to arrange for someone to kill his wife while he was establishing his alibi. But had he? And if so, why? He was said to be gentle and good-tempered. Mystery writer P. D. James, however, writing in a *Sunday Times* article, saw him as a disappointed man who could quite easily have taken out his frustration on his wife. It's no secret that women are often killed by their partner (or ex-partner).

Wallace moved to another part of Liverpool, but, weakened by the ordeal, he died soon after. No one else was ever charged with Julia Wallace's murder, and several writers were intrigued by the complexities of the strange case. James Agate wrote, "Either the murderer was Wallace or it wasn't. If it wasn't, then here at last is the perfect murder." Raymond Chandler said, "I call it the impossible murder because Wallace couldn't have done it, and neither could anyone else."

However, the writer John Gannon, himself from Liverpool, pointed the finger of guilt at Richard Parry, who had been a junior employee in Wallace's firm until he was sacked for stealing. Gannon claimed that Parry and an accomplice had set up the "R. M. Qualtrough" hoax to get Wallace out of the house, which they then broke into, killing Julia and stealing the meagre amount of money her husband had collected that day in insurance premiums.

So many years on, and despite such interest in the circumstances of that fateful night, it seems we are unlikely to ever know the truth.

THE TEENAGER AND THE LOG CABIN

When an old log cabin that had stood empty for years in Woodland Park, Colorado, was being demolished in 2015 to make way for new housing, workers made the macabre discovery of a skeleton lodged inside the chimney. Within weeks, using dental records, a forensic odontologist identified the remains as those of Joshua Maddux, who had been missing for seven years. On 8 May 2008, the nature-loving 18-year-old had set off on a walk from his father's house, but had never returned.

"One of the most traumatic things about this story is that the cabin he was found in is literally two blocks away from my dad's house," said his sister, Kate Maddux. "We looked through every part of the woods we thought he could walk to, but that cabin never came up."

The cabin's owner, Chuck Murphy, said his family bought it in the 1950s to use as a home and rental property, but it had fallen into disuse. "Occasionally, we'd go in there to check on it and there were mice and chipmunks and raccoons," he explained. "It smelled bad."

Although the remains in the chimney were confirmed to belong to the teenager, the finding didn't explain how he came to be there. Because there were no signs of trauma – no broken bones, knife marks or bullet holes – foul play was not suspected by the county coroner, who surmised that Joshua had been trying to get into the cabin by shimmying down the chimney. In his words, it "appeared to have been a voluntary act in order to gain access". The cabin's location in a wooded area with no houses very close by meant that no one would have heard any cries for help when he got stuck.

However, Murphy questioned the coroner's "accidental death" ruling, stating that he himself had built the chimney 20 years previously and had fitted the insides with thick wire mesh to keep wild animals and debris from falling down the chimney and entering the cabin. Murphy pointed out that a large wooden breakfast bar had been torn from a kitchen wall and dragged over to block the chimney from inside the cabin; and that the skeleton was found with only a thermal T-shirt. The rest of Joshua's clothes, including his shoes and socks, were folded up neatly inside the cabin.

The coroner chose to overlook these details, as well as the calls he had received naming a suspect. The accidental-death ruling was upheld: "He did come down the chimney, that's our conclusion." In response, Murphy stated unequivocally, "There's no way that guy crawled inside that chimney with that steel webbing. He didn't come down the chimney."

If, for some, the mystery of what happened to Joshua Maddux remained unsolved, his sister Kate saw it as a "miracle" that his body had finally been found as it enabled his family to give him a proper burial. All the years he was missing, they hoped he was still alive and wondered what he might be doing. "He's not lost anymore," she said. "This isn't how we wanted him to come home, but he has come home, and that's important."

DIANA, PRINCESS OF WALES: TRAGEDY IN A TUNNEL

The sudden brutal death on 31 August 1997 of Princess Diana, one of the most recognized faces in the world at the time, caused massive shock waves around the globe. The deadly high-speed car crash in a Parisian tunnel happened almost exactly a year after Diana's divorce from Prince Charles (now King Charles III) – a divorce that put an end to a 15-year marriage that had started out like a fairy tale.

A host of conspiracy theories have since purported to explain the tragedy.

As Diana drifted away from her husband and the rest of the royal family, her blossoming relationship with Dodi Fayed, son of Mohamed Al Fayed, the Egyptian owner of the London luxury department store Harrods, led to consternation in the British establishment. The fact that both Diana and Dodi were killed in the accident led to speculation that it wasn't an accident at all, but that the pair were assassinated by the British secret service as threats to the throne and the stability of the state. Their deaths would prevent the awkwardness caused by the mother of the future British king marrying into an Islamic family, possibly converting to the Islam faith and bearing more children from that marriage, perhaps encouraging her sons, Prince William and Prince Harry, to convert to Islam too.

Other conspiracy theorists claiming the accident was deliberate have implicated, among others, the IRA, the CIA, Islamic militants and the Freemasons. Evidence supporting an assassination claim is largely circumstantial but has been sufficiently compelling to warrant an official investigation seven years later.

Diana was buried quickly without a post-mortem having been carried out, despite this being a legal requirement in the UK in cases of sudden death – a fact that naturally some view as suspicious. Nothing was ever found of the white Fiat Uno that was involved in the crash.

The chauffeur, Henri Paul, has variously been said to have been drunk at the time of the crash, to have only had two drinks the entire evening, to have been driving at over 120 miles per hour, and to have been driving at 60 miles per hour (and even less at the point of impact). The fact that he had a large amount of money in a number of bank accounts led some to suggest that he was a "sleeper" agent for a secret service agency. The only survivor of the crash, who was wearing a seat belt, was Diana's bodyguard, Trevor Rees-Jones; his connections with the British military have similarly led to suspicions that he too was a "sleeper" agent for the British secret service.

Given her statement just hours prior to the crash that she was about to withdraw entirely from public life, Diana is claimed by some to have faked her own death in order to have a private life with her Egyptian lover away from the prying cameras of the paparazzi. Others explain her death as a tragically failed attempt to carry out such a plan.

UNSOLVED MYSTERIES

The verdict of the four-year-long inquest into Diana's death, which ended in April 2008, was one of unlawful killing, pointing the finger of blame at the driver, but aggravated by the pursuing paparazzi. While the conspiracy theories continue to linger years later, for many, including Dodi's father, the verdict signalled an end to the quest to explain three tragic deaths.

CHRISTOPHER MARLOWE: AN ELIZABETHAN ENIGMA

The sixteenth-century English playwright Christopher Marlowe may have lived a short life – he was only 29 when he died – but it was certainly a trailblazing one, and with much more to it besides writing plays. Likewise, there may well have been more to his death than a brawl.

Born in Canterbury in 1564, Marlowe was two months older than William Shakespeare, but he developed as a playwright rather more quickly, having written the wildly successful *Tamburlaine the Great* three years before Shakespeare even wrote his first play. He's therefore seen by some as having done much more than merely encourage the younger man, and in a recent edition of Shakespeare's *Henry VI* trilogy, Marlowe is credited as the co-writer.

But he also had a finger in several other pies, some of which could have put him in great danger, and which might have been contributing factors in his death at such a young age. Chief among these is the fact that, even while he was a student at Cambridge University, he is thought to have been a spy for Queen Elizabeth I and her government, a position that got him a helping hand with his degree (much needed, given his frequent absence from lessons), as well as enabling him to escape with no punishment after being arrested for counterfeiting coins in Holland – a crime that was punishable by death.

Various other rumours that may or may not have relevance indicate that he had been accused of homosexuality, as well as heresy for a manuscript he'd written. On 20 May 1593, little more than a year after the counterfeiting episode, Marlowe was arrested for holding heretical views after he published tracts in London opposed to the immigration of Protestants. Although his only apparent punishment was again an oddly mild one, given the nature of the crime – he was only required to check in with the Privy Council every day until further notice – just ten days later, he was killed in a brawl over the bill after dining with an acquaintance called Ingram Frizer.

Frizer, another possible government spy, supposedly stabbed Marlowe to death in the fight. But had he been put up to it by the Queen? Or did Marlowe actually meet up with three government agents that evening – agents who turned out to be assassins? Was he was murdered by Sir Thomas Walsingham, a Protestant sympathizer and agent of the Queen? Or – given his known close involvement with Shakespeare's work – did he in fact fake his own death and flee abroad to avoid being convicted of religious heresy, while continuing to write plays using a pseudonym, and could that pseudonym in fact have been... William Shakespeare?

Marlowe's alleged killer was, significantly, pardoned by the Queen, and Marlowe was buried in an unmarked grave in Deptford within 48 hours of his death. However, the inscription on the stained-glass window in the Poets' Corner of London's Westminster Abbey intriguingly includes a question mark next to the year of his death. It seems certain that the events surrounding the young playwright's death will forever remain an enigma.

THE SOUTH POLE POISONING

The extreme conditions faced by people working in Antarctica – the bitter cold, the isolation, the cramped living quarters – may have played a role in the crimes that are known to have been committed there. In 1959, a scientist at the Soviet Vostok Station murdered his chess opponent with an axe after losing to him. And in 2018, another Russian scientist was charged with attempted murder for stabbing a colleague after having an "emotional breakdown".

But whether Rodney Marks, a 32-year-old Australian astrophysicist who died on 12 May 2000 while working his second winter in Antarctica, was another murder victim, has not been determined, with many vital questions remaining unanswered.

Marks was employed by the Smithsonian Astrophysical Observatory and working on a project for the University of Chicago at the Amundsen-Scott South Pole Station, run by a US government agency, the National Science Foundation. He had a girlfriend and friends on the base, felt fulfilled by his research role and enjoyed the beauty around him.

On 11 May, Marks found he was struggling to breathe while walking between the observatory and the base. He felt tired with weak vision and tried going to bed. During a day of increasing agony and three visits to the base doctor, Marks' condition deteriorated. He vomited blood and experienced mental distress, and the doctor, Robert Thompson, unable to diagnose the problem, injected him with an antipsychotic to help calm him down. Shortly after, Marks went into cardiac arrest and died.

Given the severity of the winter climate, his body could not be flown away for an autopsy until the end of October. But those five months his body had spent on ice didn't prevent the forensic pathologist in Christchurch, New Zealand – the base for American activities in Antarctica – from discovering that Marks hadn't died of natural causes but had drunk enough methanol – a chemical used to clean scientific equipment, and highly toxic – to fill a wine glass.

So had Marks drunk it deliberately in order to kill himself? It seems unlikely, given his clear distress when he became ill. Had he drunk it deliberately to get high? He had access to plenty of alcohol. Had he drunk it accidentally? The fact that methanol is colourless and slightly sweet means it could be slipped into a drink without the victim knowing. Had one of the other 49 people working at the base intentionally spiked his drink with the lethal substance?

What adds to the uncertainty is that the investigation into the case, led by Detective Senior Sergeant Grant Wormald, took years to complete, running up against apparent reluctance by the government agency to produce the requested evidence. The National Science Foundation at last agreed to submit a questionnaire to those who had been on the base at the time, but participation was optional, and when only 13 responded, Wormald suspected some might have thought it could affect their "future employment position".

Wormald's conclusion was somewhat disturbing: "In my view it is most likely Dr Marks ingested the methanol unknowingly." In 2008, the coroner, Richard McElrea, disputed the findings of a report from 2000 that had ruled out homicide and accidental poisoning; instead, McElrea wrote that he disagreed that accidental poisoning and even foul play "can be adequately disregarded without a full and proper investigation". There was also speculation that the doctor on the station should have found the methanol in Marks' blood and treated him.

No clear picture has ever emerged of what really happened. It seemed that Marks got on with everyone at the base and no evidence ever implicated anyone there. His father, Paul Marks, accepted, eight years after his son's mysterious death, that any further investigations would only continue to come up against dead ends. "I don't think we are going to try to find out any more in regards to how Rodney died."

BRUCE LEE: DEATH BY TRANQUILIZER

Although Bruce Lee's sudden and unexpected passing at the age of 32, just as he had achieved massive success, was ultimately ruled a "death by misadventure", his iconic status and young age have fed countless conspiracy theories.

Two months before he died, the supremely physically fit American-Hong Kong martial artist and actor had been rushed to hospital with a severe headache and racked with seizures. He was treated for cerebral edema – swelling on the brain caused by a build-up of excess fluid – and returned home after a brief hospital stay. Apart from the odd headache, over the next weeks he appeared to recover well.

On 20 July 1973, he had a busy schedule, including writing to his attorney about film offers he'd received, meeting with George Lazenby, the Australian James Bond actor, to discuss his participation in Lee's latest film, *Game of Death*, and visiting the apartment of Taiwanese actress Betty Ting-Pei, with whom he was romantically involved, having recently split from his wife. When he complained of a headache that evening, Ting-Pei gave him Equagesic, a strong aspirin-based painkiller, and he went to sleep. Lee would never wake up.

The autopsy concluded that Lee had died from an allergic reaction to the tranquilizer meprobamate, the main ingredient in Equagesic. But the "death by misadventure" ruling didn't sit right with many of the superstar's fans, and soon rumours were rife about what had really killed their idol. Ting-Pei was targeted, some claiming she had deliberately poisoned him, but the theory doesn't stand up to scrutiny.

According to another source, Hong Kong Triads, rumoured to have close connections to the entertainment business, assassinated Lee because he had refused to pay them protection money, or as hired killers for another party. This source claimed they had used a delayed pressure-point attack, leaving him initially feeling fine, but with his body preparing to shut down after enough time had passed not to arouse suspicion: seemingly the perfect deadly martial-art tactic.

Others claimed that one of Lee's former martial arts teachers took revenge on him for imparting the revered ancient skills to foreigners. Still others said the US Mafia had been humiliated by Lee's refusal to become the first Asian star in Hollywood. If he was indeed the Mafia's first victim, then was his son, Brandon Lee, the Mob's second, 20 years later, when he was "accidentally" fatally shot on the film set of *The Crow* by a prop gun that was meant to be empty? Or were they both victims of the alleged Lee family curse?

Alternatively, had Bruce Lee, as some claim, been killed by a panicked prostitute after he took a powerful aphrodisiac and became violent during sex? Or was he simply a victim either of his own overly rigorous training and fitness regime or, at the opposite end of the scale, of his substance abuse?

The list of theories will likely continue to grow as further documentaries, films and books are produced purporting to tell the "true" story about Lee's untimely death.

THE BLACK DAHLIA

On 15 January 1947, a woman walking with her three-year-old daughter in a Los Angeles neighbourhood in the morning made a gruesome discovery in a vacant lot. What she initially took to be a broken shop mannequin was in fact the severed body of a brutally murdered young woman, cut in half at the waist.

The victim was 22-year-old Elizabeth Short, who had dreamed of being a film star, though she'd been working as a waitress shortly before her death. The murder has been named by *Time* magazine as one of the most infamous unsolved cases in the world, and came to be known as the "Black Dahlia murder" – possibly taking its nickname from *The Blue Dahlia*, a crime film released the previous year, while also referencing Short's habit of decorating her hair with dahlias and her penchant for wearing black clothes.

She had last been seen on 9 January getting out of a car and entering the Biltmore Hotel, well dressed in a suit, blouse and high-heeled shoes, carrying a handbag.

Although the autopsy revealed Short had died of a cerebral haemorrhage, by the time her body was found, it was completely drained of blood and washed clean, with the two halves having been arranged in a bizarre, sexual "pose", and the face slashed from the mouth to the ears to create a "Glasgow smile".

After the young woman was identified, a sordid media frenzy ensued, with one newspaper lying to Short's mother in order to elicit information. Meanwhile, there were few clues to trace the killer: a heel print on the ground, and the mutilation of the body, which hinted at medical knowledge.

On 21 January, the *Los Angeles Daily Police Bulletin*, in its call for information, showed a photograph of a glamorous, smiling, bright-eyed woman, describing her as "very attractive" and with "fingernails chewed to the quick". It noted that "she frequented cocktail bars and night spots".

Then a newspaper received a phone call from someone who claimed to be the killer, saying they would eventually turn themselves in and in the meantime would send some "souvenirs of Beth Short". A few days later an envelope was found, the address made from newspaper clippings, containing her birth certificate, address book and other personal items, all cleaned with gasoline just as the body had been, destroying any fingerprints.

Further notes were received; suspects were identified and investigated; hundreds of police officers worked on the case, and a reward was offered for information. A man named George Hodel became a more compelling suspect after his death, when his son, an LA homicide detective, accused him of killing Short and several other people.

Nothing seemed to solve the mystery definitively, however. Over the years, there have been over 500 confessions to the notorious crime, mostly by men, some of whom weren't even born at the time of the murder. In a book published in 2000, Mary Pacios, a former neighbour of the Short family, pointed the finger at film-maker Orson Welles, citing his volatile character, and the fact that in the months leading up to Short's death, Welles was making mannequins for a film that featured lacerations similar to those found on the murdered woman. Ultimately, no one was ever arrested for Short's murder.

Unsubstantiated rumours have also circulated about Short: that she was a prostitute, frigid, pregnant, a lesbian. Anne Marie DiStefano of the *Portland Tribune* wrote that: "the legend of the Black Dahlia just keeps getting more convoluted". It remains one of the LA Police Department's oldest cold case files, as well as one of the most brutal and culturally enduring crimes in American history.

DYATLOV PASS INCIDENT

Was it an encounter with angry aliens? A savage yeti attack? More than 60 years after nine highly experienced Soviet hikers frantically cut their way out of their tent in the northern Ural Mountains one freezing February night in 1959, theories continue to circulate as to what happened. Because none of them survived to tell the tale.

The hikers were graduate students from the Ural Polytechnic Institute. Poignantly, photos survive of their final days, showing the group as happy, confident, enjoying their break in the wilderness.

When it was realized that they had gone missing later that month, a search party found six bodies that had succumbed to hypothermia, while the remaining three showed signs of massive physical trauma, including a fractured skull and a crushed chest and broken ribs. Two of them had their eyes missing, one had a missing tongue, and one had missing eyebrows. Most of the bodies were nearly naked, the warm clothing having been left in the tents. Those who were clothed seemed to have taken clothing from the bodies of others. They seemed to have been fleeing something.

The medical examiners' report concluded that although most had died from frostbite and hypothermia, an "unknown compelling force" had killed the remaining three, whose injuries were similar to those sustained by car-crash victims. But beyond that, no further explanation was forthcoming as to what the "compelling force" might have been. The case was abruptly closed, all the documentation being ordered to be sealed.

The closure of the case in this way fed the speculation, which kicked into an even higher gear when some of the hikers' clothes and the campsite itself were found to contain extremely high levels of radiation. During their funerals, some of the bodies were said by family members to have given off an unnatural orange glow, and some hair had gone grey – both signs of exposure to radiation.

So had the hikers strayed into a nuclear testing zone? The Russian authorities' denial that any such testing had been going on in that area didn't convince everyone.

But others claimed that the strange orange orbs seen in the sky for several weeks during that period had been evidence of UFOs, somehow responsible for the strange deaths. One investigator noted that treetops around the hikers and their tents were charred and burned.

The possibility that an angry indigenous tribe had murdered the hikers – the Mansi call the area "The Mountain of the Dead" – for trespassing on their lands was eliminated as the injuries on three of the bodies were deemed to be more severe than any human could have inflicted. That didn't completely rule out a yeti attack. One other much-discussed theory was that some of the hikers were undercover KGB agents who were scheduled to meet with an American party for a "controlled delivery" – an exchange of contraband.

But perhaps the most likely explanation is that the nine victims were trying to escape from a "slab avalanche", which would have made loud cracking and rumbling noises as it fell across their tent. As experienced hikers, they conducted a textbook emergency evacuation, attempting to head to an area away from the avalanche. If so, the missing eyes, tongue and eyebrows must have happened later.

Sadly, according to Douglas Preston, summarizing the findings, less experienced hikers might have remained near the tent, dug it out, and survived. "But avalanches are by far the biggest risk in the mountains in winter, and the more experience you have, the more you fear them. The skiers' expertise doomed them." The avalanche theory was given in 2020 as the official cause of the incident, named after the party's leader, Igor Dyatlov.

THE PAINTING AT WEMBLEY POINT

A mysterious oil painting left at a café table is one of the few clues to the identity of a young Black woman who plunged 21 storeys to her death. But two decades after she was found dead in the river under Wembley Point, a tower block in London, on 29 October 2004, investigators have been unable to fathom who she was.

Wembley Point (now called the WEM Tower London) is known to have hosted art exhibitions in the past, and there were also a number of company offices in the building. The café was on the twenty-first floor. At the table believed to have been vacated by the Wembley Point Woman, as she has become known, were a packet of Marlboro cigarettes, a lighter, a *Guardian* newspaper, a bus pass issued on Seven Sisters Road, a black carrier bag – and a colourful, somewhat abstract oil painting depicting a number of faces and figures around an enigmatic blank space where a face should be.

Some witnesses claimed to have seen the woman in a distressed state in the tower-block lift. She was aged between 20 and 40, of average height, and wore a maroon bomber zip-up jacket, black trousers and boots, a black leather glove on her right hand, and silver rings on her left. However, despite an image of what the woman looked like being released on the eighteenth anniversary of her death, no one has ever come forward to identify her, and investigators are no closer to finding out who she was, or why she died in the way she did.

Dave Grimstead, from Locate International, a charity focused on solving missing-person cases, said, "When we look into old cases… there are a few things that always need answering: where, when and how the person died and who they were. What's unusual here is that we know the answers to almost all those questions. The only thing we don't know is who Wembley Point Woman is, or how she came to be at that location at that time."

The unknown woman, whose body was found in the River Brent that flows past Wembley Point, today lies in an unmarked grave in a cemetery near Watford, on the outskirts of London. With nothing having come to light in 20 years to give investigators any clue as to what might have driven her to jump from the top of a high-rise, sadly she looks likely to remain there.

ROBERT MAXWELL: DEAD IN THE WATER

In life, Robert Maxwell was regarded by many as a flamboyant example of rags-to-riches success: as a poverty-stricken Jewish survivor of the Nazi occupation of his native Czechoslovakia, he made his way to the UK, where he served in the Second World War, became a publisher, a member of Parliament, and a wealthy and globally influential press baron with a lavish home in Oxford and connections at the highest levels. In death, he's remembered mainly as a fraudster, a suspected spy, and the father of Ghislaine Maxwell, convicted for crimes related to sex trafficking.

His death on 5 November 1991 was a murky affair, occurring with no witnesses, the day after a tempestuous argument with his son Kevin. It concerned a meeting Robert Maxwell was supposed to have with the Bank of England over his failure to pay back £50 million in loans. Instead of attending the meeting, he continued with plans to go sailing near the Canary Islands aboard his superyacht, the *Lady Ghislaine*.

Maxwell's last contact with the ship's crew was at 4.45 a.m. on 5 November, when he demanded that they turn up the air conditioning in his cabin; by lunchtime he couldn't be found anywhere and was reported missing. Twelve hours later, a Spanish fisherman spotted his naked body floating in the Atlantic Ocean, 15 miles from his yacht. No wounds were found except for a slight graze on one shoulder. The three pathologists who performed post-mortem examinations on Maxwell each came to a different conclusion about the circumstances that led to his death.

According to one, he died of a heart attack. Another agreed that he had suffered a heart attack, but said he fell into the sea as a result and drowned. A third claimed he had simply toppled into the ocean and drowned while urinating overboard, as was his habit. The last explanation was the one some members of his family leaned towards – even in the face of a flood of conspiracy theories concerning the demise of the man whose business empire was on the brink of collapse.

It transpired that Maxwell had used hundreds of thousands of pounds from his companies' pensions funds to finance his corrupt business practices and rich lifestyle. As a result, thousands of his employees would lose their pensions. A BBC documentary series in 2022 revealed he was increasingly paranoid as he bugged the offices of his media empire and kept the tapes in a suitcase. Did he know his number was up while he was sailing in the Atlantic that day?

His son Ian said, "I think it is highly unlikely that he would have taken his own life, it wasn't in his makeup or his mentality." In 1954 he'd been declared insolvent, and in 1971 declared unfit to run a public company. He'd come back from those disasters, so it seemed strange that he would have felt so differently this time.

Maxwell was suspected by the British Foreign Office of being a double agent, or even a triple agent, and he had known links with MI6 (the British secret intelligence service), the Soviet KGB and the Israeli intelligence service, Mossad, leading some to think his death was an assassination by Mossad agents because he was threatening to expose Israeli state secrets. However, Ian Maxwell said, "I don't think any murder conspiracy stands up. So for me, it is an unexplained accident, and I'm content to live with that."

JEFFREY EPSTEIN: DEATH BEHIND BARS

In 2008, American financier Jeffery Epstein was convicted by a Florida state court of soliciting a prostitute and of procuring an underage girl for prostitution. Having served almost 13 months in custody for those offences, though with work release, he was arrested again in July 2019 on federal charges for the sex trafficking of dozens of minors in Florida and New York, some as young as 14.

While awaiting trial, he was imprisoned in the Metropolitan Correctional Center in New York City. On the morning of 10 August, he was found unresponsive in his cell, in a kneeling position on the floor, with a strip of bedsheet wrapped around his neck and tied to the top of his bunk. He was taken to the New York Downtown Hospital, where he was pronounced dead, and the city's chief medical examiner ruled his death a suicide by hanging.

Epstein's lawyers, however, were quick to challenge the ruling and launched their own investigation, which resulted in them claiming that the evidence in his cell and from the autopsy was more indicative of homicidal strangulation – that is, that Epstein didn't kill himself; rather, his lawyers said, he was murdered. This claim was bolstered by the numerous standard prison procedures that had been violated in the run-up to and aftermath of his death and by the fact that Epstein, who had links with many powerful people, including Donald Trump and Bill Clinton, had claimed to have compromising information about famous individuals.

In the days after his incarceration, following a suspicious incident when he was found semi-conscious, Epstein had been placed on suicide watch in an observation cell for six days. He was then returned to a Special Housing Unit where he would have a cellmate and guards would check on him every 30 minutes. But on 9 August, his cellmate was transferred and no replacement arrived. The two guards assigned to check on his cell apparently fell asleep and then falsified records. Meanwhile, two cameras in front of Epstein's cell malfunctioned.

The claim that Epstein was murdered spawned scepticism in the American public over the official ruling, as well as multiple conspiracy theories. A poll conducted shortly after his death found that only 29 per cent of American adults believed he committed suicide, while 42 per cent thought he was murdered to prevent him from spilling the beans on the famous people he claimed to know too much about. The remaining 29 per cent were undecided. By 2020, a majority of Americans believed Epstein was murdered. An alternative murder theory proposed that he had been silenced by co-conspirators or other participants in his sex crimes.

There were also those who falsely claimed that the images allegedly showing Epstein's body being transported to hospital were actually images of a body double, pointing to differences between the body's ear and that of Epstein in a juxtaposed photo – which turned out to be one of a teenage Epstein, so that any differences were more likely to be the result of ageing. Nevertheless, this claim continued to be promoted on social media, together with the equally false theory that Epstein was alive and well and living at his ranch in New Mexico.

Epstein's brother, Mark, also rejected the possibility of suicide, saying, "I could see if he got a life sentence, I could then see him taking himself out, but he had a bail hearing coming up."

Ultimately, however, whether Epstein took his own life or someone else took it for him (the answer to which may never be known), as the leaders of the House Judiciary Committee pointed out, the death of this "high-profile and – if allegations are proven to be accurate – particularly reprehensible individual while in the federal government's custody... has allowed the deceased to ultimately evade facing justice".

JILL DANDO: MURDER ON THE DOORSTEP

The murder of the popular British TV personality Jill Dando at the age of 37 in 1999 shocked a nation still reeling from the death less than two years previously of Princess Diana, to whom she'd often been compared, in terms of looks and age. Dando was originally from a seaside town in Somerset, and at the time of her death was living in central London and was one of the best-known faces on TV, co-presenting the unsolved-crimes TV programme *Crimewatch*.

She was shot at point-blank range outside her house in Fulham, London, late on the morning of 26 April when she was returning home. As she approached the front door a man grabbed her from behind, forced her to the ground and put a 9 mm-calibre semi-automatic pistol to her head, firing one shot that killed her instantly. Her neighbour, on hearing a scream, looked out of his front window but didn't realize what had happened. He did, however, see a white man, aged around 40 and about six feet tall, walking away from her house – the only definite sighting of her killer.

The largest murder inquiry ever launched by the Metropolitan Police – and the UK's biggest since the hunt in the 1970s for the serial killer known as the Yorkshire Ripper – got under way.

In July 2001 a local man, Barry George, who had a history of stalking women, was convicted of Dando's murder, mainly on the basis of a single particle of gunpowder found in the pocket of one of his coats. However, doubt was later cast on the validity of this evidence. According to forensic scientist Angela Shaw, "A single particle a year later in a coat pocket could not link Barry George to the shooting", and seven years later George was acquitted of Dando's murder.

The police identified over 2,000 potential suspects in the case, including the Serbian warlord Arkan, as Dando had fronted a BBC appeal for aid for refugees fleeing ethnic cleansing in the Balkans. Her killing could have been in retaliation for the NATO bombing of the Serbian television headquarters – a key propaganda tool for Serbian leader Slobodan Milošević – that left 16 employees dead. The day after Dando's murder, another BBC employee received a death threat from a man claiming to be a Serbian activist who said that he had killed Dando. By the time Arkan was identified as a suspect in 2012, he was already dead himself, but the fact that Dando's killing was never publicly claimed by a credible source throws doubt on the theory that it was a politically motivated attack.

Another possibility is that, given Dando's work on *Crimewatch*, she could have been a victim of a London gangland killing as a warning to others not to take on organized crime. But despite all the cases she'd been involved with and the number of concerned criminals who might have been at large, the senior investigating officer, Hamish Campbell, said, "We examined all the [*Crimewatch*] cases that

Jill was involved in, which cases she broadcast... [and] there was simply no evidence for it."

One of the other main theories was that Dando was killed by a stalker or an obsessed fan. It had been used in the case against George. Shortly before her death, Dando had announced her engagement to the man she had been dating for just over a year, so jealousy could have been a motive for her murder; she had apparently spent the previous night at her fiancé's home. However, while 140 people were identified by the police as having an unhealthy interest in Dando, all were finally eliminated as suspects.

Quarter of a century after the shooting, Campbell has admitted that he doesn't think Jill Dando's killer will ever be found and brought to justice.

REEVA STEENKAMP: BLOODY VALENTINE

On 14 February 2013, 29-year-old Reeva Steenkamp was shot four times through a locked toilet door by her boyfriend of three months, Oscar Pistorius, at his home in Pretoria, South Africa.

Steenkamp was a paralegal with a successful career as a model, having featured in *FHM* magazine and being the face of Avon cosmetics in South Africa. She also campaigned against bullying and was preparing to talk to girls at her former school about gender-based violence.

Pistorius was slightly younger, a world-famous Paralympic athlete whose feet had been amputated when he was a child, and who enjoyed playing with guns. He said what happened was a terrible accident, that he believed the person locked in his toilet must be a dangerous intruder who'd broken in; not his girlfriend, who'd either got up to use the toilet without waking him or – according to some – was cowering inside the tiny room following a violent argument with him.

Although former partners and friends of Pistorius would later testify to his previous controlling, abusive behaviour with women and reckless use of guns, at his first trial, the jury found him not guilty of murder but guilty of the lesser charge of culpable homicide.

His case was helped by the mishandling of the crime scene by the police, who were found to have contaminated and "lost" crucial evidence, including a valuable watch. One of the officers in charge of the case resigned when it emerged that the toilet door through which Pistorius fired four lethal Black Talon expanding bullets had almost immediately been removed from the crime scene, allegedly because of concerns that corrupt officers would sell photographs of it to the media.

Pistorius was sentenced to five years in prison, but only served ten months.

In December 2015, the Supreme Court of Appeals overturned the culpable-homicide verdict and found Pistorius guilty of murder. However, even though under South African law murder carries a minimum sentence of 15 years, Judge Masipa only sentenced him to six years. Two years later, the Court of Appeals extended the sentence to 13 years and five months, with the possibility of parole in 2023.

Steenkamp's mother has said she believed her daughter had been too scared of Pistorius to take their relationship to the next level and was thinking of ending it; if that's true, then tragically, she left it too late.

ALEXANDER LITVINENKO: TAINTED TEA

When the Russian dissident Alexander Litvinenko died in a London hospital on 23 November 2006 after languishing there for three agonizing weeks, sushi took a nosedive in popularity as it was initially thought he had consumed contaminated raw fish at a sushi restaurant in Piccadilly, in the heart of the UK capital.

However, raw fish was let off the hook once the cause of death was found to have been rather more sinister – Acute Radiation Syndrome (ARS) induced by the ingestion of lethal, though hard-to-detect, Polonium-210. It was now thought that the deadly dose had been slipped into a cup of tea at the Millennium Hotel's Pine Bar in Grosvenor Square, the finger of suspicion pointing to the Russian men he was with at the time. High polonium contamination was later found there.

Litvinenko himself was a former agent of the Federal Security Service of the Russian Federation (FSB), the main successor to the Soviet KGB. After being arrested for publicly accusing his superiors of ordering the assassination of the Russian oligarch Boris Berezovsky, he had defected to the UK in 2000. During his years in England, Litvinenko, who coined the term "mafia state", wrote two books that were openly critical of the

Russian president, Vladimir Putin. On his deathbed, he directly accused the president of being the "person responsible for my present condition".

Russia turned down a demand by the British government for the prime suspect in Litvinenko's poisoning, Andrey Lugovoy, to be extradited to stand trial in the UK, leading to strained relations between the two countries. However, in 2011, Litvinenko's widow, Marina, following a vigorous campaign through the Litvinenko Justice Foundation, finally won the right for an inquest into her husband's death to be conducted by a coroner in London.

After several time-consuming setbacks, the coroner eventually concluded that Litvinenko's murder had been carried out by Lugovoy and a second suspect, Dmitry Kovtun, and that they were "probably" acting under the direction of the FSB, with Putin's approval. The European Court of Human Rights established "beyond reasonable doubt" that Russian agents Lugovoy and Kovtun had procured the rare poison, and made several attempts to poison Litvinenko.

What enabled the truth to be found was that Litvinenko hung on to life for three weeks after the poisoning, long enough to make accusations that would lead to the polonium and its source.

MARILYN MONROE: SOMETHING'S GOTTA GIVE

When the iconic film star Marilyn Monroe died in August 1962 at the age of 36, her death, from an overdose of a cocktail of barbiturates, was ruled suicide. But more than 60 years later, an air of mystery still surrounds the events of the night the troubled actress was found dead in her Los Angeles home.

Born Norma Jean Baker in 1926, Monroe had a difficult upbringing in a variety of foster homes, some of them abusive. She started working as a model in the 1940s and when her "blonde bombshell" looks brought her to the attention of film directors in the 1950s, she became hugely successful.

Yet the shallow roles she was given based solely on her "sex appeal", a succession of short-lived marriages, and even her superstar lifestyle, made her increasingly unhappy. She was plagued with ill health and her behaviour became ever more erratic; she ended up being fired from the last film she ever made, the 1962 film with the title that now seems ironic: *Something's Gotta Give*.

Monroe's disturbed state of mind when she died made suicide a likely cause. But was it the real cause? Although they were covered up at the time, she is now known to have had affairs with the then-president of the US, John F. Kennedy, and his brother, Attorney General Robert Kennedy: were they somehow involved in her demise?

In 1982, the Los Angeles District County Attorney reopened the investigation, and journalist Anthony Summers tape-recorded 650 interviews as he conducted his own research to present a case in a biography a few years later. Interviews with federal operatives showed intelligence agencies worried about the leaking of information.

John Kennedy had already ended his relationship with Monroe. Was he concerned that his spurned former lover would not only reveal their affair, but also pass government secrets to communists she was associated with, connected to the Cuban leader, Fidel Castro? Or had Robert Kennedy, as Monroe's housekeeper Eunice Murray later claimed (though her reliability has been questioned), visited Monroe on the night of her death and quarrelled with her?

Much remains unknown about Monroe's final moments, as well as about what happened immediately after. The speculated time of death varied between 11 p.m. on the night of 4 August (according to the widow of Monroe's publicist, Arthur Jacobs, who asserted in a documentary interview that her husband was alerted that something was wrong while they were at the Hollywood Bowl) and 3 a.m. the following morning (according to the housekeeper). In fact, according to the paramedics who were called to her house, she was comatose but not dead when they found her, dying later in the ambulance, and her body then being brought back home.

She was found unresponsive in her bed next to a bottle of sleeping pills, the telephone left off the hook. Other empty bottles of pills were scattered around the room. Did FBI agents swoop in to clean up her house or arrange the scene before anyone else got there, having been informed about her death?

Speculation continues, and details from various accounts often differ wildly. As Monroe said herself, "The true things rarely get into circulation. It's usually the false things." People claiming to know the truth about the film star's tragic demise will likely continue to surface.

CLEOPATRA: DEATH ON THE NILE

History has it that Cleopatra, the last pharaoh of Egypt, died at the age of 39 from the poisonous bite of an asp, which she administered to her breast in an act of suicide, the snake having been delivered hidden in a basket of figs. But did she really?

Most of what is known about Cleopatra – and inspired artists, Shakespeare and Hollywood film-makers – came from her enemy Octavian, and was written down as historical fact nearly 200 years after her death in 30 BCE by the Roman writer Plutarch. And even he acknowledged that no one could be certain about how she died, and that in fact there were no signs on her body that were consistent with a snakebite having caused her death: "Neither spot nor other sign of poison broke out upon her body. Moreover, not even was the reptile seen within the chamber, though people said they saw some traces of it near the sea." Cleopatra's two handmaidens, Iras and Charmion, were found dead with her, both also having apparently succumbed to snakebites.

However, as some historians have pointed out, the asp – regarded as a symbol of divine royalty, and also known as the

Egyptian cobra – is a very long snake, measuring between 5 and 8 feet in length, and thus would have been difficult to conceal in a small fig basket. Further, if Cleopatra wanted to kill herself, an asp bite, while being extremely painful, would not necessarily have been deadly. As biographer Stacy Schiff wrote, "A woman known for her crisp decisions and meticulous planning would surely have hesitated to entrust her fate to a wild animal."

Others are sure that Cleopatra used some other means to dispatch herself. "It is certain that there was no cobra," claims Christoph Schaefer, a professor of ancient history, who leans towards a mixture of hemlock, wolfsbane and opium as Cleopatra's more likely poison of choice.

That, of course, presupposes that she did die by suicide. Octavian, her rival for dominance in Egypt, had plenty of reasons to want Cleopatra dead, and is regarded by some as a suspect. Indeed, after her death, he is known to have ordered the murder of Caesarion, her son by Caesar, who would have been her successor to the Egyptian throne. Cleopatra had fought her way to power and would certainly have feared being taken prisoner. Given the deadly politics of the day, political intrigue throws up many possible scenarios.

What isn't in dispute is that Cleopatra met her end nine days after the death of her lover, Mark Antony, who is said to have fallen on his own sword, having been falsely informed that Cleopatra had been killed. When he then received word that she was in fact still alive, he was carried to her, and died in her arms. What happened during the next nine days is unlikely ever to be known. The dead lovers were, by Cleopatra's request, laid to rest together near the Egyptian city of Alexandria – but exactly where, like so much else about Cleopatra's final days, remains a mystery.

In the words of Plutarch, "The truth of the matter no one knows."

DEADLY PERFUME

Charlie Rowley had just moved into a new flat and was thriftily furnishing it with items he had bought cheaply at charity shops, and even with things people had thrown away that were still in good condition. It was in that foraging frame of mind that the resident of Salisbury in the English county of Wiltshire came across a perfume box in a litter bin.

Rowley said he found the perfume bottle wrapped in cellophane in a sealed box and kept it. On 30 June 2018, he gave it to his girlfriend Dawn Sturgess. The 44-year-old mother of three sprayed her wrists with the perfume.

What happened next, according to Rowley, happened very quickly. Having fixed the spray nozzle on the bottle and come in contact with the oily substance, he went to wash his hands. His girlfriend, meanwhile, started complaining of a headache and went to lie down in the bath. He found her fully clothed in the bath and very unwell. He was able to call a friend, who phoned the emergency services, but then he too started to feel ill and his mouth began to foam.

The couple were rushed to hospital and the police declared a major incident, as it was not known where the contamination had come from or how widely it had spread.

Tragically, Sturgess died a week later. Her boyfriend was treated in hospital for three weeks, spending some of that time on a ventilator and unconscious. "When I woke up and came off the ventilator a doctor explained that Dawn had died," he said. "I couldn't take it in. The police explained the perfume contained novichok."

It turned out he'd unearthed a crucial piece of evidence police had been searching for.

In the same city in March, a 66-year-old former Russian agent Sergei Skripal and his daughter Yulia had been found unconscious on a bench. When under investigation, it was discovered that they had been poisoned by the nerve agent novichok, which had been smeared on their front door handle. The fact that the perpetrators of the attack had disposed of the poison in a litter bin helped the crime to be solved.

"Unwittingly, I'd done something the police hadn't managed in three months... I'd found the novichok bottle," explained Rowley.

Skripal and his daughter both eventually recovered, as did DS Bailey – the police officer who became ill after going to their home to investigate the attack – although he was consequently unable to continue working as a police officer. Later in 2018, two Russian intelligence officers, Anatoliy Chepiga and Alexander Mishkin, were suspected to have conducted the poisoning. A third agent, Denis Sergeev, was later also named.

A spokesperson for the Russian Foreign Ministry in 2021 said, "We decisively reject all of London's attempt to blame Moscow for what happened in Salisbury."

The British Crown Prosecution Service authorized charges but they could not be formally made unless the suspects were arrested. With no extradition treaty with the UK, none of the three suspects was thought likely ever to face a trial in a British court.

Rowley's contaminated flat and all his belongings had to be destroyed after the deadly incident. But that was the least of his worries. His feelings of guilt for having accidentally poisoned his girlfriend continued to haunt him. "I didn't mean to, but I killed my girlfriend," he said. "How do you ever get over that? I can't. I want justice for Dawn. I want people to be caught, but I don't expect that to happen."

EDGAR ALLEN POE: NEVERMORE!

A man is found wandering deliriously in soiled clothes that do not belong to him. What's more, he cannot or will not relate how he happens to be in that city, which is not his own. It reads like the opening to a story by Edgar Allen Poe, credited by many as the inventor of detective fiction, and a master of the macabre and mysterious.

In fact, it's a true account of one of Poe's own last few days alive. Shortly after this, he died at the age of 40, racked with hallucinations and repeatedly calling the name of someone who was never traced. And around 175 years after Poe's strange demise on 7 October 1849, his cause of death remains as much a mystery as it was back then.

Poe, soon to be married to Sarah Elmira Royster, had set off from his home in Richmond, Virginia for Philadelphia to edit a friend's poetry collection. He never arrived and no one saw him until six days later, when he was found in an incoherent state in a stranger's dirty apparel outside a pub in Baltimore, Maryland.

He had Baltimore connections: he'd had stories published there, and had briefly held a post as an assistant editor, before he was fired for drunkenness; he had procured a marriage licence in Baltimore and lived there for a while. But that day all he was apparently able to communicate to the man who found him was the name "Joseph E. Snodgrass" – an editor friend of his with some medical training. A note was sent to Snodgrass, reading: "There is a gentleman, rather the worse for wear, at Ryan's 4th Ward polls, who goes under the cognomen of Edgar A. Poe and who appears in great distress, and he says he is acquainted with you, and I assure you he is in need of immediate assistance."

Snodgrass came quickly but was unable to do more than get Poe to the local hospital, where he fell into a raging fever. For four days he called out the name "Reynolds" over and over, though no one connected to Poe knew anyone of that name, nor have historians since found a Reynolds connected with Poe. He also referred to his wife in Richmond, though his first wife had been dead for a year and he had not yet married Royster.

When he passed away, his official cause of death was given as phrenitis – swelling of the brain – though this has been questioned, with several other causes suggested, some more sordid than others, from rabies to syphilis. The medical records were lost, and the man who wrote his obituary was his arch-rival, who cast him as a lunatic and later as a drug addict.

Some (including Snodgrass) claimed at the time that Poe drank himself to death. Poe was known to have been unstable and turned to drinking after his wife's death. But in the months before his death, had been almost teetotal.

A small, hard object found inside Poe's skull when his coffin was temporarily exhumed later suggested a possible brain tumour. A more sinister notion involves foul play by his fiancée's family, who didn't want the marriage to take place.

Another theory put forward in 1872 said he was forced to consume alcohol for the purposes of "cooping", a type of electoral fraud that involved kidnapping citizens and making them drunk, then escorting them to a polling station to vote for a particular candidate, sometimes several times dressed in different outfits. This would explain much about Poe's condition.

As to whether there will ever be a satisfactory explanation for Poe's strange death, the answer is probably not. Or, as his supernatural creation the Raven was fond of saying, "Nevermore!"

A MYTHICAL
MENAGERIE

You may think that sightings of the yeti are just abominable rumours. But there's a whole, fascinating field of study reserved for creatures whose existence is disputed or unsubstantiated. It's called cryptozoology.

This chapter looks at such creatures, and at the people who have in some cases devoted their entire lives to solving the mystery of whether they truly exist – such as the man who's been camped out on the shores of Loch Ness since the early 1990s hoping to make an undisputed sighting of the creature said to be lurking in its depths.

You'll read of black "uncanny" shapes, blood-curdling cries, things that slither or growl in the night, or pull you down into the deep, and a baby cursed to be the Devil. Some monsters, like Spring-heeled Jack, attacked vulnerable young women. Some of the creatures have fictional counterparts – Count Dracula, for instance. But as you'll read, there might be other bloodsucking beasts around that attack animals, puncturing their skin and drinking their blood. Keep a clove of garlic close by, though, just in case...

Bigfoot and the Bunyip, among others, have legendary status; myths may have originally emerged to explain forces of nature or to warn people away from danger. Some of them, explainable as hoaxes, we can now look upon with humour – but for whoever saw or thought they saw one, the encounter could have been truly terrifying.

THE CREECH HILL
BULLBEGGAR

A hill topped by a clump of trees in the rural English county of Somerset may sound quintessentially peaceful, but at close quarters, it may be anything but – at least, if you make the mistake of disturbing its resident Bullbeggar...

"Bullbeggar" is the local term for a bogeyman, and the one residing on Creech Hill, near the small town of Bruton, has a reputation for being particularly malicious towards anyone who approaches its territory. There's been plenty of human presence on the hill in the past, both living and dead, including archaeological evidence of an Iron Age hill fort in the first millennium BCE. The highest part of the hill is known as Lamyatt Beacon, the site of a Roman-period Celtic temple containing a statue of Mithras or Mars, and many offerings were found there. In Saxon times it was a burial site, and the whole area is rich in history, being along the old drovers' road from Glastonbury.

In the 1880s, so the story goes, two bodies were unearthed while the hill was being used as a quarry for the extraction of minerals. That's when its former use as a cemetery was revealed, and thereafter, it was haunted by a "black uncanny shape" sometimes referred to as a "black dog", and by the sound of invisible footsteps.

The Bullbeggar had arrived, and from then on it jealously guarded its hilltop domain. Legend has it that one night when a farmer cut across the hill on his way home from the market, it lay prone in the road, pretending to be unconscious. When the kindly farmer offered his assistance, the sinister figure shot up and chased the terrified man home, hammering on the walls of his house and screaming, and then bounding away laughing like a maniac when the farmer's family came to his rescue.

On another occasion, the Bullbeggar is said to have attacked a traveller on Creech Hill, rising up in front of him as a swirling, shapeless black mass while letting out a blood-curdling scream, and forcing the stranger to fight for his life all through the night using an ash branch. As the sun rose the next morning, the Bullbeggar faded away, and the man made a swift escape, never to return that way again.

Some local residents remain convinced that a human-shaped malevolent presence continues to haunt Creech Hill. In 2014, a man who lives at the foot of the hill said, "We regularly hear these chilling screams late at night and I have also seen the tall, gaunt hunched-shouldered man walking through the path in trees [sic]."

Whether the Bullbeggar really exists is anyone's guess. But for anyone happening to find themselves near a tree-topped hill in south-east Somerset, forewarned is forearmed...

LOCH NESS MONSTER: MESSING WITH NESSIE

Does a huge marine creature really lurk in the depths of Scotland's largest loch? Surprisingly, that question has been bobbing around for at least 15 centuries, and doesn't seem to be in any danger of floating away. Even confessions of hoaxes and the fact that no compelling evidence has ever surfaced to prove (or even disprove) the existence of anything more than an oversized eel inhabiting Loch Ness haven't put "Nessie" hunters off.

Mythology around dangerous creatures lurking in deep waters was not unusual in Northern Europe in the Dark Ages. The loch reaches a depth of 260 yards, which could easily have harboured great sea serpents, and misty conditions only add to the intrigue. Ancient stone carvings found nearby depicted a mysterious beast with flippers. The first written mention of such a creature was in a seventh-century biography of St Columba, which told of how in 565 CE, a monster attacked a swimmer but was ordered by the saint to "go back". For the next 1,000 years or more, only occasional sightings were reported.

The legend blossomed again in the twentieth century, however, when in 1933 a couple claimed to have seen something resembling a "dragon or prehistoric monster" crossing the newly completed lochside road as they drove along it, only to vanish into the depths.

Once their story was printed in a Scottish newspaper, others came forward to declare they had spotted the legendary creature, prompting the *Daily Mail* to latch onto the monster frenzy and commission a Nessie-hunter, Marmaduke Wetherell, to investigate. Big-game hunter Wetherell soon claimed to have found large footprints on the shore of the loch that he believed belonged to "a very powerful soft-footed animal about 20 feet long". Zoologists, however, determined that the tracks had been made (though not necessarily by Wetherell) with a hippopotamus-footed umbrella stand or ashtray.

The fraudulent footprints did nothing to dampen international ardour for Nessie, and the following year a photograph emerged appearing to show a monster with a small head and neck, leading to speculation that the creature was a plesiosaur, a marine reptile that became extinct over 60 million years ago. The photograph wasn't exposed as a hoax for another 60 years, when it was revealed that the "monster" had a plastic and wooden head that had been attached to a toy submarine.

Steve Feltham's fascination with finding Nessie started in 1970 when, as a seven-year-old, he went on a family holiday to Scotland and visited the "Loch Ness Phenomena Investigation Bureau". The team of volunteers conducted round-the-clock surveillance of the loch. On his "nessiehunter" website, Feltham writes: "What really caught my imagination was the platform they had built, on which they had mounted a cine camera and tripod; the lens alone must have been a metre long. Grown men looking for monsters? Fantastic."

The fact that the bureau was wound up seven years later, having failed to come up with any substantial evidence, didn't put Feltham off. As an adult, he continued to visit the loch, having become totally hooked on the quest. In 1991, he sold his house and took up residence in a van on the shores of Loch Ness – where he remains to this day and continues to watch, living proof that Nessie hunters at least are alive and well.

While neither sonar nor DNA has been able to prove the existence of a monster, in a loch that contains more water than all English and Welsh lakes together, who knows what may still be there, hiding from the hunters?

CHUPACABRA: THE MEXICAN HAIRLESS GOAT-SUCKER

The name "chupacabra" – Spanish for "goat-sucker" – was coined by the Puerto Rican radio DJ Silverio Pérez following a series of bizarre attacks on livestock on the Caribbean island of Puerto Rico in 1995. The victims – goats, sheep and other farm animals – had been found dead, drained of their blood but the carcasses left uneaten.

Such killings had first been reported, with the bodies bled dry through small incisions, in 1975 in the small town of Moca. The strange slaughter was initially thought to be evidence of a satanic cult. However, in 1995, when sheep were discovered drained of blood, with puncture wounds, it was soon put down to the chupacabra, even though no actual specimens of the creature were found, putting it firmly in the ranks of bloodsucking beasts along with vampires.

Since then, sightings have been reported in several other countries in the Americas, including Argentina, Brazil, Peru, Mexico and the south-western US. In 2018, reports came from India of suspected chupacabra attacks and sightings, and in October 2019 it was blamed for the deaths of some chickens in Puerto Rico, where chupacabra hysteria had first exploded a quarter of a century before.

As to what a chupacabra looks like, it depends who you ask. Some say it resembles a large reptilian kangaroo, standing upright, and with huge red eyes. Others insist it's a four-legged, hairless beast the size of a small bear, with spines running along the ridge of its back, bulging eyes, fangs and claws. Still others, especially in the American Southwest, depict it as more dog-like.

Perhaps unsurprisingly, the chupacabras resembling dogs in the American Southwest were found to be exactly that – mange-ridden coyotes, their condition leaving them with little fur, thickened skin, and so weak that they only had the strength to attack easy prey such as livestock and rabbits. Likewise, the chupacabras in India were thought to have probably been street dogs, and some of the Mexican sightings turned out to be of xolos, also known as Mexican hairless dogs.

Meanwhile, at least one sighting is itself thought to have taken its inspiration from a 1995 science-fiction horror film. One of the original Puerto Rican eyewitnesses revealed later that she "believed that the creatures and events she saw in *Species* were happening in reality in Puerto Rico at the time". Her description of the chupacabra she blamed for killing livestock is nearly identical to the alien creature Sil that features in the film. Furthermore, the accounts of creatures having been bled dry were later found to have been exaggerated and inaccurate.

Whatever the reality, the chupacabra does seems to have clamped its bloodsucking fangs firmly into the Latin American imagination.

A FISHY TALE

The famous statue of the "Little Mermaid" sitting on a rock by the waterside in Copenhagen, Denmark, was inspired by the Danish author Hans Christian Andersen's 1837 tale of a young mermaid willing to trade her life in the sea for a human soul. But belief in the legendary half-human, half-fish sea creatures goes back very much further than that, with their portrayal in Stone Age cave paintings dating back 30,000 years.

In folklore, mermaids and mermen are often associated with bad luck and doom: when they're not luring sailors to a watery death, they're summoning storms and sinking ships. In Greek mythology, the sirens, who appear in Homer's epic poem *The Odyssey*, were three seductresses who were originally half-bird and half-women, but were later depicted as being more mermaid like, with fish tails, using their sweetly treacherous singing to tempt love-struck seamen to get closer and closer until they were finally dashed to pieces on the rocky coastline. The Greek god Triton, too, is often portrayed with a fish-like tail.

In the ancient Far East, mermaids were cast as the wives of powerful sea-dragons, communicating on their behalf with the emperors on land. In the Middle East, the Islamic Golden Age folk-tale collection *One Thousand and One Nights* described mermaids as having "moon faces and hair like a woman's but their hands and feet were in their bellies and they had tails like fishes", and the Syrian goddess Atargatis was a half-woman/half-fish deity. The mythical African water spirit Mami Wata is also often portrayed as a mermaid.

On the other side of the world, the Aboriginal people of Australia referred to mermaids as "yawkyawks", possibly in reference to their siren-like mesmerizing songs, and in Japanese legend, merfolk called kappa, with ape-like faces and tortoiseshell backs, are said to live in watery places and to have an appetite for children, lone swimmers and, oddly, fresh cucumbers.

In the Middle Ages, mermaids were depicted in art as real sea creatures alongside whales and fish. Tales of encounters with mermaids were told as true stories – such as the seventeenth-century Dutch folk tale in which a mermaid was injured entering Holland through a dike, and nursed back to health in a nearby lake, becoming a productive Dutch-speaking Catholic citizen able to perform useful household chores.

This belief in mermaids was fed in the nineteenth century by hoaxes, such as the showman P. T. Barnum's popular attraction the "Feejee Mermaid". People paid 50 cents to see what to modern eyes would have been an obvious fake – top half monkey, bottom half fish – but at the time, many were intrigued by their first sight of a "real" mermaid.

The US's National Ocean Service (NOS) website states: "No evidence of aquatic humanoids has ever been found." Human-size ocean-dwelling animals such as dugongs, with their mermaid-like forked tails and flippers resembling short arms, may have been responsible for the widespread belief in mermaids and mermen that persists to this day. As recently as 2009, a mermaid was claimed to have been sighted off the coast of Israel, performing a few tricks for onlookers before disappearing into the sunset. A $1 million reward was offered for the first person to photograph the creature, but as yet the reward remains unclaimed.

VAMPIRES: STICK YOUR NECK OUT...

Mercy Brown grew up on her father's farm in Exeter, Rhode Island, and like many other members of her family, in 1892, Brown died of tuberculosis, at the age of 19. But she was singled out as the scapegoat to explain the deaths of all the others.

Brown's body was examined by the local townspeople, and when it didn't show signs of severe decay (unsurprisingly, as she had been dead for less than two months and the icy New England winter would have slowed down decomposition), they accused her of being a vampire. To kill her "properly", they cut out her heart, burned it, and then fed the ashes to her sick brother, who, probably as a result, died soon after.

Scholars trace belief in vampires back to a fear that the dead could harm the living. Vampirism was connected with disease, and stopping the vampire was seen as a way of controlling the spread of it. The people of Exeter were not alone at the time in believing that vampires truly existed. Without recourse to science, they became convinced that certain diseases, including porphyria, tuberculosis and rabies, were linked to the bloodsucking creatures, and that vampires' first victims were their own families. In 2006, the skull of a sixteenth-century plague victim in Venice was found with a brick in its mouth to prevent feeding on others after death.

Count Dracula is perhaps most people's idea of the stereotypical vampire – darkness-seeking, intent on finding innocent necks to plunge his thirsty fangs into. While Bram Stoker's legendary character from his 1897 novel was fictitious, Stoker is thought to have been inspired by Vlad III (Dracula), a cruel fifteenth-century prince of Transylvania, also known, chillingly, as "Vlad the Impaler". He probably took further inspiration from the Hungarian Countess Elizabeth Báthory, who is thought to have murdered up to 650 young women at the turn of the seventeenth century in a bid to preserve her own youth by bathing in or drinking their blood.

Although the history of vampires goes back many centuries (stories were told in ancient Greece and medieval Europe of creatures that drank the bodily fluids of their victims), it was the Gothic literature of the eighteenth and nineteenth centuries that gave birth to vampires as we know and loathe them today. Ranging from grotesque to supremely beautiful, most vampires are depicted as having pale skin – perhaps as a result of being "undead" (that is, existing somewhere between dead and alive). That may also be why many of them are said to be unable to cast a shadow, or to be photographed or recorded on film.

The one thing all vampires have in common, though, is their thirst for human blood, typically utilizing their sharp fangs to syphon off their victim's blood, thereby turning them into vampires too. People can also become vampires through sorcery, contagion or suicide, or from a cat jumping over their corpse. Once a person has become a vampire, it's hard to get rid of them. Garlic, crucifixes, running water and holy water will ward them off, but driving a wooden stake through their heart or exposing them to sunlight are the most well-known methods of dispatching vampires for good.

People calling themselves vampires exist today – "sanguinarians" who drink the blood of willing donors in private, or "psychics" claiming to feed off the energy of others. Today, however, it's a group people choose to belong to, showing a discretion and consideration very unlike vampires of yesteryear.

THE BUNYIP: WITH FLIPPERS, FANGS AND FEATHERS, IT MUST BE A KANGAROO!

In the murky swamps and billabongs of south-east Australia lurks the legendary bunyip. Active at night, the bunyip is said to feast on humans, whose blood-chilling cries can be heard echoing up from the dark inland waters. The name, which came from the Wemba-Wemba Aboriginal people of Victoria, means "scary monster" or "evil spirit", and European settlers recorded that the Aboriginal people had a real fear of the creature.

Some describe the bunyip as having the size and appearance of a dog, while others say it resembles a seal, with flippers, or something between a bird and an alligator. Some say its colour is glossy black, others dusky grey. In still other tales, it's as big as a horse, with horns, shaggy fur, scales or feathers, and with fangs or tusks, and either one or two eyes...

Although the bunyip first appeared tens of thousands of years ago in Aboriginal stories of the Dreamtime when the world was created, sightings were also reported by the first

233

English settlers in Australia in the early nineteenth century. In 1933, Charles Fenner suggested a possible explanation: that seals sometimes made their way up rivers, and southern elephant seals or leopard seals would have made strange and ominous cries.

The bunyip has continued to loom large in the Australian imagination, featuring in everything from films and songs to books and paintings. Today, scientists think that if such a beast ever truly existed, it is likely to have been a now-extinct giant wombat called a "diprotodon", a water-dwelling marsupial that lived in Australia 20,000 years ago. As for the haunting cries drifting up from the lagoons, they put those down to the calls of the bittern marsh birds.

Others, though, think the early Europeans settlers may have simply been dumbfounded by their first sight of kangaroos. To people who had never set eyes on marsupials before, these powerful leaping native creatures of eastern Australia must have seemed mysterious, mystical, and worthy of being taken for the legendary bunyip. Even without flippers, fangs or feathers.

CAN YOU SCOTCH
THE SASQUATCH?

Does a giant ape-like creature really roam North America? The plethora of alleged sightings of Bigfoot (or Sasquatch, as the creature is also known) might suggest that there could indeed be something large and hairy out there. There have, after all, been 10,000 reported glimpses in the last 50 years alone.

Most of these sightings have been in the north-western region of North America, where – perhaps not coincidentally – there are also many indigenous legends linked to the creature. The word Sasquatch itself is derived from "sasq'ets", which means "wild man" or "hairy man" in the language used by some Salish First Nations peoples in south-western British Columbia, Canada.

One of the earliest newspaper reports of a "gorilla type" creature was a story of one being captured in the Victoria area of Canada in 1884. This sparked a barrage of accounts of further sightings – 1,340 in total through the nineteenth and twentieth centuries – but most of them were later revealed to be hoaxes.

Then in 1958, a Northern California newspaper, *The Humboldt Times*, reported that gigantic footprints had been discovered near Bluff Creek, California. The writer of the story referred to the creature that had allegedly made them as "Bigfoot" – setting off a wave of Bigfoot mania across the country.

By the time the footprints were revealed to have been a hoax by a man called Ray Wallace, whose children outed him after his death in 2002, there was no putting the creature to bed. Bigfoot had become firmly established in popular culture across North America, and reports of sightings continued to flood in, usually describing the creature as up to 10 feet tall and covered in hair.

The most famous video footage purporting to show Bigfoot was taken in 1967 by Roger Patterson and Bob Gimlin. Though the film quality is poor and jerky, it appears to show a large and hairy two-legged ape-like creature striding through a clearing and then turning to look at the camera. It was never exposed as a hoax, but the likelihood is that it was simply a human wearing a costume.

In the years since then, film technology has made huge strides forward in terms of the clarity of videos and photographs – yet, strangely, any images taken of Bigfoot remain blurry and out of focus. Does this simply mean that Bigfoot spotters are consistently bad photographers?

Audio recordings of mysterious growls, shrieks and other noises, including strange wood-knocking sounds, have also been claimed to be evidence of the hairy monster's existence. Despite some biologists saying they could have been made by a wolf, a YouTube video of howls and screams recorded in a forest in north-western Ontario went viral in 2019. Hair, faeces, skin scrapings and blood claimed to have come from Bigfoot have in most cases also been shown to be bogus, having actually come from cows, racoons, deer, bears and even humans.

So, when it comes down to it, there is no hard evidence for the existence of Bigfoot. The fact that no one has ever seen the creature's face, coupled with the biological reality that such a creature would need to have reproduced at some point in its long history (meaning there would need to be at least two Bigfeet at any one time, and remains of some of them should have been found), likewise points firmly in the direction of monstrous myth.

But that doesn't mean Bigfoot won't continue to be seen and heard from time to time.

SPRING-HEELED JACK

Spring-heeled Jack terrorized Victorian England for more than 60 years. The devil-like figure who allegedly attacked women across the country occupies a place that's somewhere between urban legend and disturbing reality.

The creature first sprang to the attention of the public in 1837, when a young female servant was set upon on Clapham Common in London, her attacker ripping her clothes and gripping her tightly with what she described as claws that felt "cold and clammy as those of a corpse".

Although the Lord Mayor remained sceptical, given the number of stories of ghostly apparitions on the streets of London at the time, soon letters were flooding in with similar stories of women being attacked all over London by the same creature, described as having eyes like balls of fire and hands like icy claws, spewing blue flames from his mouth, and with the ability to leap from rooftop to rooftop.

In 1838 the Lord Mayor received a letter of complaint from an anonymous resident of Peckham claiming that a servant girl had answered the doorbell to a "no less dreadful figure than a spectre... The consequence was that the poor girl immediately swooned, and has never from that moment been in her senses." The writer believed the attacks were the result of a nasty bet;

a person seemed to be going around in a haunting disguise with claws on his hands, causing hysteria. The Lord Mayor instructed the police to search for the person (or persons) responsible for what he termed a "pantomime display", with a reward offered. Even the elderly Duke of Wellington armed himself and set out on horseback.

But the attacks continued, and spread further afield. During the 1850s and 60s, Spring-heeled Jack, as the by-now legendary creature had long been named by the press and the public, put in appearances in Northamptonshire (where he was described as "the very image of the Devil himself, with horns and eyes of flame"), Lincolnshire and Devon. In East Anglia, his modus operandi altered somewhat, with drivers of mail coaches being his main target. In 1870, he was said to have leaped on top of a military sentry box at the Aldershot Garrison in Hampshire, terrifying the guard inside. According to some reports, the soldier shot at the strange figure with no effect, claiming that he then disappeared into the darkness "with astonishing bounds".

The last sightings of Spring-heeled Jack were in north-west England between 1888 and 1904 – when he was just as agile, seen bounding down the streets of Everton in Liverpool, leaping between the rooftops and the cobbles, evading capture for the final time.

Henry Beresford, the eccentric 3rd Marquess of Waterford, is generally accepted as having been behind the elaborate creation of Spring-heeled Jack, possibly in revenge for humiliating encounters with a woman and a police officer. He was known for his drunken antics, brutal jokes and destructive behaviour, his vandalism with a pot of red paint one night in 1837 giving birth to the phrase "painting the town red". But the man known as the "Mad Marquis" died in 1859, so there were clearly some copy-cat pranksters too.

Real or not, many Victorian children were warned to be good or Spring-heeled Jack would leap up to their bedroom window and peer in at them...

BEWARE THE GROOTSLANG

A massive, vengeful, gem-hungry serpent with a body as bulky as an elephant is believed by terrified locals to dwell deep in a diamond-filled cave known as the Bottomless Pit or Wonder Hole, in the middle of the Orange River in Richtersveld, South Africa.

The Grootslang (Afrikaans for "big snake"), which is thought to be up to 39 feet long, apparently has diamonds in its eye sockets and scales as black as night, and gives off a pervading sense of evil. It is thought by the local Khoekhoe people, as well as by some white settlers, to take cattle from the banks of the river and to have the task of guarding its treasure for eternity. Despite its cruel streak, the Grootslang is said to be willing to bargain with its victims if they will part with enough precious gems in return for their lives.

In 1917, the English businessman Peter Grayson embarked on a treasure hunt in the Richtersveld diamond-mining area, saying, "I am determined to return to England as a very rich man or a dead man." His greed may have been his undoing, as after other members of his party were attacked and injured by lions, leaving him alone on his quest, he subsequently vanished, his disappearance linked by some to the Grootslang. Indeed, according to legend, only one person who has entered the

Wonder Hole has ever returned. That man – a prospector – was so disturbed by the overpowering smell of sulphur inside, and by the cloud of bats that flew at him, that he had to be pulled back up on a cable winch and never went into the cave again.

In 1949, there were reports of a black-haired, finned monster the size of a bull, with a long neck and fins. Two people claimed they dragged such a beast out of the water and left it on shore, but it crawled back and disappeared before their story could be corroborated. The following year, local people talked of seeing a huge snake on the Orange River, and a black serpent's head was seen in the water with a large body. Other sightings from 1960 referred to two "huge, strange" long and thin creatures swimming across the river.

Some have speculated that the legend of the Grootslang originated with sightings of pythons, which are native to South Africa, and which can grow to 26 feet in length. As for its diamond-encrusted eyes – well, in the world of legendary creatures, some things simply don't have any rational explanation!

SEARCHING FOR THE YETI

In 1986, while hiking in the Himalayas, Anthony Wooldridge took two photographs of a shape that he claimed to be a yeti. The photographs were analyzed and declared genuine – to the delight of yeti and Bigfoot believers across the globe. Sadly, it was subsequently discovered that Wooldridge had simply mistaken a dark outcrop of rocks for the creature.

There is broad agreement among those who've claimed to have seen one about what a yeti looks like: muscular, covered in dark grey or reddish-brown hair, weighing between 200 and 400 pounds, and standing on two legs at around 7 feet tall. There's agreement, too, as to where it lives: in the mountains of Asia, below the snow line. But despite umpteen explorations of remote mountain regions of Russia, China and Nepal, no one so far has been able to prove that the yeti really exists.

The yeti started life as a dangerous character in the ancient legends and folklore of the people of the Himalayas, the word "yeti" being derived from a compound of the Tibetan words for "rocky place" and "bear". Alexander the Great demanded to see a yeti after conquering the Indus Valley in 326 BCE, but was fobbed off by the locals with the excuse that such a creature would be unable to survive at such a low altitude.

The name by which it's commonly known in the West, "Abominable Snowman", came about through an error in translation. Sherpas attributed some large footprints discovered on an expedition in 1921 to a creature they referred to in Tibetan as "metoh-kangmi", meaning "man-bear snow-man". The British journalist Henry Newman mistranslated "metoh" as "filthy", but then, in his newspaper report, modified it to the apparently less offensive term "abominable", inadvertently giving a new name to the legend.

Reported sightings of the yeti in the twentieth century included one in 1951, when Eric Shipton, while attempting to climb Mount Everest, photographed some large prints in the snow. These are arguably the best evidence to date for the creature's existence – though some say they were less exotic prints simply distorted by the melting snow. Although Sir Edmund Hillary and Tenzing Norgay also reported seeing large prints during their successful scaling of the mountain in 1953, both men would later become more sceptical of yeti sightings.

The history of yeti sightings is replete with misidentification. In 2011, a finger kept in a monastery in Nepal, where it had been revered as having belonged to a yeti, was shown by DNA analysis to actually be human, possibly from the corpse of a monk. In 2017, nine specimens of bone, tooth, skin, hair and faeces allegedly coming from yetis were analysed in a laboratory. Eight were shown to have come from bears, and one from a dog.

But the true believers remain undeterred, claiming that the lack of hard evidence only goes to show how rare and elusive the yeti is – seemingly not abominable at all, but, on the contrary, rather touchingly shy and reclusive.

PULLING THE RUG FROM UNDER THE BEAST OF BODMIN

Does a large panther-like wild cat with white-yellow eyes roam the remote granite tracts of Bodmin Moor in the English county of Cornwall? Sixty or more sightings since 1983 and numerous reports of mutilated livestock say it might. And in 1995, just when the British government, having ordered an official investigation into the question of its existence, concluded that there was no verifiable evidence either for or against the beast being real, three young brothers came across a leopard skull on the banks of the Cornish River Fowey. Speculation now ran wild. Had the creature escaped from a local zoo? And had it been the vicious cattle killer?

Neither turned out to be the case. Somewhat disappointingly, the skull was determined by the British Museum to have most likely come from an imported leopard-skin rug...

But that damp squib didn't put an end to sightings of the beast, many by holidaymakers in the area, and three years later, video footage emerged of a 3-foot-long black cat spotted on the moor. Described by the curator of Newquay Zoo as "the best evidence yet" in favour of the beast's existence, it was among new information submitted to the government for further consideration, though in stills captured from the video, the creature looks very like a domestic cat.

If Bodmin Moor does indeed have its very own beast, as many continue to firmly believe it does, where did it come from? Three pumas were claimed to have been released into the wild by Mary Chipperfield following the closure of her zoo in Plymouth in 1978, so is there actually more than one beast? If so, how did the bleak conditions and lack of a consistent food supply on the moor sustain the pack? Or is there just one beast, the sole remaining member of a species thought to have long become extinct in Britain?

Alternatively, is the beast of Bodmin Moor something altogether more spooky – the ghost of a creature that roamed the area back in the mists of time? Reports of hissing and growling and, more disturbingly, of something that sounds like a woman screaming lean towards a paranormal explanation.

The questions won't go away – and neither, it seems, will the fresh sightings and pawprints. One Plymouth resident, who captured a few pictures of a black puma-like cat crossing her garden, said, "I guess it remains a mystery."

KRAKEN: MONSTER AT SEA?

The superpower of the octopus-like kraken, Norway's legendary sea monster, is its enormous size. Said by some sailors to be the length of ten ships, while others put it at a mile and a half long, it's rumoured to have lured mariners to their doom when they mistook it for an island. As soon as they landed on it, they found themselves being sucked into the bubbling sea when the gigantic creature suddenly rose up.

The first description of it was in a Scandinavian travelogue by the Italian writer Francesco Negri in 1700, who wrote of a huge fish with many arms. Although in some early accounts, the beast is described as having spindly, crab-like legs, it was more usually likened to a massive octopus, and it's thought that sightings of giant squid, which can grow to 50 feet long, might have reinforced the legend of the mighty kraken.

They certainly gave rise to a long-running argument in the middle of the nineteenth century between a ship's captain and the biologist Sir Richard Owen (the man who invented the word "dinosaur"). When the captain claimed to have encountered a 60-foot sea monster while sailing the *Daedalus*, Owen was certain that what he had actually seen was merely a seal. The captain retorted that he knew full well what a seal looked like, and that this creature certainly wasn't one. The dispute continued over similar sightings until 1873, when a fisherman caught a giant squid, and Owen had finally to acknowledge the existence of something that looked very much like the kraken.

Superstitious sailors often became concerned while sailing in northerly oceans if the water around them started bubbling, taking it as a sign that the kraken was about to emerge from its depths. But bubbling water is also a classic sign of underwater volcanic activity, particularly in the seas around Iceland. However, given that the highly respected eighteenth-century zoologist Carl Linnaeus may have described the kraken as an actual living organism in his 1735 treatise *Systema Naturae*, while Bishop Erik Pontoppidan also described it in his 1750s *The Natural History of Norway*, it's hardly surprising that these sailors fully believed they were about to be engulfed by a monstrous invertebrate rather than by a tsunami caused by a submarine volcanic eruption.

The myth continued when French novelist Victor Hugo wrote of it, influencing Jules Verne's depiction of the kraken in *Twenty Thousand Leagues Under the Sea*. Verne used the term also to mean a giant squid. There were references in Alfred Tennyson's poetry and Herman Melville's *Moby-Dick*.

The discovery towards the end of 2022 of a new variant of the Covid-19 virus that was then given the name of the legendary monster of the deep ensured that the kraken won't be sinking beneath the waves any time soon. It's also the name of a cryptocurrency, giving rise to a whole different type of speculation...

BRUNCH WITH THE JERSEY DEVIL

In 1939, the US state of New Jersey declared its very own official state demon. The creature was known only too well to Walter Edge, who was governor of the state twice, and who once said, "When I was a boy... I was never threatened with the bogeyman. [Instead,] we were threatened with the Jersey Devil, morning, noon, and night." Whether Governor Edge ever actually laid his eyes on the Jersey Devil is not known.

Some say the Jersey Devil was the thirteenth child born to a New Jersey Quaker woman known as Mother Leeds in 1735. The impoverished woman cursed the unwelcome addition to her already sizeable brood, crying out that the child would be the Devil – as, indeed, it turned out to be. Although the baby had a normal appearance when it was born, it transformed into a creature with hooves, a goat's head, bat wings and a forked tail. Mother Leeds kept the child confined to the family home until one day it flew into a rage, growling and screaming and beating everyone in the house with its tail. Then it flew up the chimney and headed into the Pine Barrens, a desolate swampy region in the south-east of the state, where it made its home.

Over the past 250 years, countless folk – including Napoleon Bonaparte's brother, Joseph – have allegedly seen or heard the creature on its nightly wanderings, a Republican judge even claimed to have sat down to a ham and egg breakfast with the Jersey Devil. Other people's close encounters with him led to disaster however: crops failed, cows stopped giving milk, livestock were mutilated, and droughts brought famine to the area, all, apparently, on account of the Jersey Devil, who was said by some to appear every seven years.

In one week in 1909, newspaper reports of a sudden flurry of around 30 sightings of the Jersey Devil across several states resulted in panic, as the myth seemed to be morphing into reality. Scientific explanations were sought, with some experts claiming that the creature was a leftover Jurassic dinosaur that had somehow survived in limestone caves.

In more recent times, sightings of the Jersey Devil have tailed off as the remote pine habitat said to be its home has become more developed and the roads better lit. In 2015, however, video footage went viral of what was claimed to be a Jersey Devil taking off into the sky, having initially been mistaken for a black llama in the middle of the road.

So, despite admirable efforts to put an end to the devilish creature – over the years, it's been exorcized, electrocuted, shot, burned, and declared both officially dead and officially foolish – the Jersey Devil seems to live on. This could be good news for any bounty hunters out there: the $10,000 reward offered by Philadelphia Zoo for the Jersey Devil's capture in 1909 was put in the shade by a whopping $250,000 offered a few decades later, and it hasn't yet been collected...

OUT OF
THIS WORLD

Although the term "unidentified flying object" (UFO) wasn't coined until the middle of the twentieth century, the tantalizing idea of aliens from other planets visiting us here on planet Earth has been around for almost as long as humans themselves.

This chapter looks at such cases from all over the world – some dating back many years, even many centuries, while others are much more recent. During the Cold War of approximately 1945 to 1990, when the then Soviet Union was pitted against the US and its allies, UFO sightings became much more common. The anxiety and paranoia generated by all the secret goings-on, both on the ground and in space – not to mention the plethora of Hollywood science-fiction films suddenly being made depicting humanity under attack from hostile aliens – piqued people's imagination and led to "flying saucer" becoming almost a household term.

Sometimes there was clearly a more worldly explanation for what were taken to be extraterrestrials. Some were exposed as elaborate hoaxes, and some were simply cases of mistaken identity. But in some other instances, despite the sceptics and naysayers pouring scorn on them, the documented evidence was compelling, and those who don't believe or want us to be the only living species in the universe continue to read it as proof that we are indeed not alone.

So, are we or aren't we? Read on and decide for yourself...

BARNEY AND BETTY HILL: THINK OF AN ALIEN, ANY ALIEN...

The stereotypical image of an alien – long, thin body; elongated head; large, slanted black eyes – owes itself to an alleged extraterrestrial encounter on a deserted mountain road in September 1961.

Barney and Betty Hill were driving home from a belated "honeymoon" road trip through Montreal and Niagara Falls. They had reached the White Mountains of New Hampshire when they became aware of a strange white light in the night sky. Barney was sure it was just a satellite, but it seemed to be moving towards them. They pulled over at a picnic spot, Betty took a look through binoculars and said what she saw was spinning.

When, 70 miles later, the bright light started hovering above them, Barney grabbed his handgun, jumped out of the car and ran into a field to get a clear view.

What he saw took his breath away: a jet-sized spacecraft shaped like a pancake, with grey uniformed beings staring out at him through rows of windows.

He ran back to the car and, without telling his wife why, jammed his foot on the accelerator. The last thing either remembered before losing consciousness was the sound of loud rhythmic beeps at the back of the car. Two hours later, they both came to, having somehow made it 35 miles down the road, but with no memory of how they had got there. When they finally arrived home, they felt disturbed and dirty, and looked dishevelled – Barney's shoes were scuffed, Betty's dress was ripped and their watches had stopped.

Although Betty immediately threw herself into research about UFO sightings, it wasn't until 1964 that the couple, both of whom had subsequently developed symptoms of anxiety, sought help from a psychiatrist who specialized in hypnosis. During their sessions with him, the full account emerged of what Betty and Barney claimed had actually happened to them during those missing two hours.

The noise at the back of their car had been the alien craft landing on their vehicle, in the process putting them to sleep in order to transfer them into the pancake-shaped spacecraft. There, they were each examined in detail – Betty even claiming that a crude pregnancy test was carried out on her. The following year, the Hills' incredible story was picked up by a Boston newspaper, and went on to become the subject of a best-selling book and a major film.

Harvard psychologist Richard J. McNally said: "The 'alien-abduction' phenomenon, in my opinion, shows how sincere, non-psychotic individuals can develop beliefs about, and false memories of, incredible experiences that never happened."

Sleep paralysis and hallucinations have also been suggested as possible explanations – indeed, the couple admitted to being tired before they even set out on the drive home. Alternatively, as a mixed-race couple living in a predominantly white state at a time of extreme civil-rights unrest, could they have suffered another kind of attack?

The couple's psychiatrist, for his part, concluded that Betty had dreamed the abduction and Barney had absorbed her story. However, the Hills never wavered from their story, and Betty became well known in the field of UFO research.

FALCON LAKE INCIDENT: PROSPECTOR STRIKES UFO GOLD

Amateur geologist Stefan Michalak's alleged sighting of an unidentified flying object at Falcon Lake, Manitoba has been described as "Canada's best-documented UFO case". It happened on 20 May 1967 during a trip to Whiteshell Provincial Park, where he was prospecting in the wilderness for quartz and silver. Michalak was suddenly startled by a flock of geese that became agitated by something near the lake.

In the account he sold soon after to *The Winnipeg Tribune* newspaper, Michalak, who had emigrated to Canada with his family from Poland, said that it turned out to be two cigar-shaped hovering objects emitting a red glow. One of them landed, and he sketched it in detail before approaching it to investigate, assuming it to be a secret military aircraft but seeing no identifying insignia. Michalak, an industrial mechanic by trade, claimed to hear voices inside, but when he attempted to communicate – first in English, then in Russian, Polish and German – there was no response.

Donning the welding goggles he used while prospecting for protection, he walked to the doorway and looked inside the craft, where he saw light beams and flashing panels, but otherwise it appeared empty. As he drew back, three panels slid the door shut, and when he touched the outside it was so hot the fingertips of his gloves melted. The craft rotated, and a grid of holes blasted heated gas at him, leaving a grid-like burn mark on his chest and setting his shirt and cap alight. Then it flew away.

He ripped off the flaming clothing and – after a brush with a highway patrol officer who believed he was drunk although he didn't smell alcohol – returned to his motel room, by which time he was feeling nauseous. The doctor wasn't available at Falcon Lake, so he returned home to Winnipeg by Greyhound bus. There, he was admitted to the hospital emergency room to be treated for his injuries and other symptoms, which included diarrhoea, headaches, blackouts and continued weight loss. Though test results came up negative, his physical condition was reportedly consistent with radiation poisoning. His son Stan, nine years old at the time, recalled a strong smell of "sulphur and burnt motor" coming from him.

Going public with the story led to massive interest, visitors and calls. Michalak, a down-to-earth former military policeman, came to regret having said anything about the incident, maintaining to his dying day that the UFO was an experimental aircraft and that he'd never claimed it was of alien origin, but simply wanted to warn others of the possible danger.

The report by the Royal Canadian Mounted Police (RCMP) was unable to explain Michalak's physical injuries or the 15-foot circle of burned vegetation. Tests found a high level of radiation at the site. The official conclusion by the bodies involved in the subsequent investigation, including the United States Air Force, was that the case was "unexplained".

Sceptics put Michalak's burns down to an alcohol-related accident or an allergic reaction, and, pointing to inconsistencies in the story he told the highway patrol officer, suspect that it was merely an attempt to discourage rival prospectors from straying onto his site.

Michalak died at the age of 83 in 1999, but despite his own reticence and the scorn poured on his story by some, the Falcon Lake UFO incident has lived on in the Canadian imagination. In 2018, in commemoration of its 50th anniversary, the Royal Canadian Mint issued a $20 non-circulating silver glow-in-the-dark coin featuring the incident as part of its "Canada's Unexplained Phenomena" series. The owners of the Falcon Beach Ranch offer tours of the location of what has been described as "the world's most documented UFO sighting".

MEDIEVAL UFOS

The news of the day in the middle of April 1561 was of strange objects seen in the sky by the inhabitants of Nuremberg, today a city in Germany, then an independent city-state in the Holy Roman Empire.

According to a printed broadsheet article with accompanying illustration by Hans Glaser, at dawn, men and women witnessed what some UFO researchers have since interpreted as an early sighting of extraterrestrial beings.

First, blood-red arcs appeared in the rising sun. Soon, blood-red crosses and globes were seen, and rods. Then some kind of aerial conflict took place with erratically moving globes, crosses and rods fighting for more than an hour. The spectacular show was followed by what seemed to be a crash-landing in clouds of smoke somewhere beyond the city limits, whereupon a spear appeared pointing from east to west.

Glaser produced the woodcut engraving of the scene, complete with a detailed description of what took place:

> ...These all started to fight among themselves, so that the globes, which were first in the sun, flew out to the ones standing on both sides, thereafter, the globes standing outside the sun, in the small and large rods, flew into the sun.

Besides the globes flew back and forth among themselves and fought vehemently with each other for over an hour. And when the conflict in and again out of the sun was most intense, they became fatigued to such an extent that they all, as said above, fell from the sun down upon the earth "as if they all burned" and they then wasted away on the earth with immense smoke. After all this there was something like a black spear, very long and thick, sighted; the shaft pointed to the east, the point pointed west...

The event was scarcely mentioned for four centuries, until the Swiss psychologist Carl Jung included it in his 1958 book *Flying Saucers: A Modern Myth of Things Seen in the Skies*. Since then, scientists have come up with various explanations, including the possibility that what the citizens of Nuremberg witnessed were "sundogs" (or "parhelia"), natural meteorological phenomena formed by sunlight being refracted through ice crystals high up in the atmosphere.

Alternatively, it could have been an early firework display. The first European book to describe the preparation of pyrotechnics (Vannoccio Biringuccio's *De La Pirotechnia*) had been published the previous year.

As far as Glaser was concerned, though, there was no earthly explanation for the bizarre scene. "Whatever such signs mean," he wrote, "God alone knows." He added that we should see such miracles as signs from God and that we should repent and mend our lives.

THE MARFA LIGHTS: CATCH A FALLING STAR

West Texas is known for its ubiquitous oil wells and the vastness of its rugged desert landscape – as well as for mysterious glowing balls of light... They were first reported in 1883 by a cowhand, who saw flickering lights one evening while driving a herd of cattle near Mitchell Flat, an area east of the town Marfa. Although he – and other settlers who had seen similar lights – assumed they were from Apache campfires, no ashes or any other signs of fires were found.

Decades later, during the Second World War, pilots at nearby Midland Army Air Field also spotted the lights but were unable to discover their source. Other eyewitnesses, before and since, have called them ghost lights, weird lights, strange lights, mystery lights and Chinati lights (from the nearby Chinati Mountains) – and have described them as being a variety of colours, including white, red, blue and yellow. They are said to usually fly above the desert vegetation but below the level of the background mesas, and as either hovering, merging, twinkling, dividing into two, flickering, floating upwards or darting across Mitchell Flat.

The Marfa Lights only appear sporadically, on a handful of nights a year, but when they do make an appearance there's no shortage of explanations as to where they've come from – with some even questioning whether they actually exist at all.

If they're not evidence of visitors from outer space, they might just be, according to Native American legend, fallen stars. Still others say they are the wandering ghosts of Spanish conquistadors. There are more mundane explanations, too. Some scientists put them down to the glow of vehicle headlights from nearby US Highway 67 (though, of course, neither Highway 67 nor motor cars existed back in 1883, when the lights were first reported). Or they might be a "Fata Morgana", an optical illusion resulting from a layer of still, warm air resting above a layer of cooler air – a common condition in the West Texas desert – causing something to appear to float.

Alternatively, they could be glowing will-o'-the-wisps produced by methane lurking among the substantial oil and gas reserves in the area. Or caused by electricity generated by geological activity. The only undisputed fact in all of this is that no one knows for sure. And that, unlike many strange sightings in the sky, they continue to appear.

So, are the Marfa Lights merely an optical illusion, the spectacular result of some kind of natural process, or are aliens (or ghosts, or stars) making an illuminating appearance in the remote West Texas desert? Why not take a trip to the official Marfa Lights Viewing Area 9 miles east of Marfa, and decide for yourself?

ROSWELL: THE ULTIMATE COVER-UP?

In the summer of 1947, a rancher discovered wreckage on his property 75 miles north of Roswell in the US state of New Mexico. With extraterrestrial fever running high at that time (the term "flying saucer" had been coined just months before, following a sighting in Washington state), he believed the remains – that included rubber strips, tin foil and thick paper – to be from an alien spacecraft. The commanding officer of the Roswell Army Air Field appeared to confirm the rancher's suspicions, releasing a statement in which he described the find as a "flying disc".

This only stoked the national hysteria, with reports surfacing from eyewitnesses who claimed to have seen alien bodies being removed from the crash site. Moreover, a teletype operator in Albuquerque working for a group of local radio stations claimed that as she was putting reports of the crashed flying saucer on air, her machine seized up and the following anonymous message mysteriously appeared instead: "Do not continue this transmission!"

The government was increasingly seen as trying to cover up the truth, and indeed very quickly made a U-turn: the debris, officials now stated, was rather more mundane, being a crashed weather balloon, several of which had previously come down in the area.

This abrupt rebuttal of the previous "flying-disc" explanation left many paranormal researchers sceptical, but it wasn't until 1994 that the US Air Force admitted that the "weather balloon" story had been false, in a bid to cover up the true nature of the wreckage. It was in fact, it now claimed, part of a spy device from a classified project – Project Mogul – aimed at detecting sound waves over the then USSR. As for the alien bodies, a follow-up report in 1997 explained that these were actually fallen parachute-test dummies.

To some, these two reports resolved the Roswell mystery once and for all. Others, however, were not so sure. Donald Schmitt, co-founder of the International UFO Museum and Research Center in Roswell, contended that if the flying saucer had simply been a story to divert attention away from the truth, it was counter-productive, likely to create more interest in that area where the US military was conducting covert operations, including atomic bomb trials.

Meanwhile, another theory circulated, perhaps even more outlandish than the alien claims: that the wreckage was actually part of an experiment devised by Soviet leader Joseph Stalin and Nazi concentration camp doctor Josef Mengele, whereby adolescent children had been deliberately deformed by the Soviets to resemble aliens and then flown to New Mexico, where they would disembark from the craft and be mistaken for Martians, causing widespread hysteria that would lead to America's early-warning radar system being flooded with other UFO sightings. Soviet records, naturally, contain no evidence of any such experiment.

OUT OF THIS WORLD

To this day, the town of Roswell remains defined by the events of 1947, with a flying saucer-themed McDonald's, streetlights resembling aliens, and even a model of an outer-space family stranded in a broken-down UFO on the side of US Route 285. It seems the flying-saucer story hasn't quite gone away – perhaps it never will.

THE TODMORDEN ABDUCTION

An unexplained death and 25 missing minutes led to a sleepy West Yorkshire market town becoming a UFO hotspot in the summer of 1980. This event would also change forever the life of a local policeman.

On 9 June 1980, PC Alan Godfrey was sent to investigate the strange death of a coal miner who, having vanished while walking to the local shop, was found three days later on top of a coal heap in Todmorden, 20 miles from his home. PC Godfrey described the man's hair as having been "roughly cut" and reported mysterious burns on his neck, head and shoulders – burns that the coroner would confirm had been treated with an unidentifiable "strange ointment". Godfrey later said that the miner looked like he'd been frightened to death, his eyes wide open.

Although no definitive cause of death was ever given, theories circulated as to what had happened, including that he had been murdered by the KGB – the 56-year-old man's name was Zigmund Adamski and he was born in Poland; his wife believed he might have been kidnapped. Others said he had been struck by ball lightning – or that he had had a fatal encounter with extraterrestrial beings.

The story would have been terrifying and bizarre enough if it had ended there. But five months later, the same policeman, on his way to deal with an early-morning call about escaped cattle, claimed to have spotted a large diamond-shaped craft rotating in the sky above him and emitting a bright light.

The line was dead when Godfrey tried to call the incident in to the station from his car. And then, suddenly, the object vanished in a vivid flash and the policeman found himself over 30 yards further down the road, still sitting in his vehicle. He saw that his watch had moved on 25 minutes from when he'd glanced at it moments before, and that his boot was split open and there was an itchy mark on one of his feet. On going back up the road, he found it was completely dry even though it had just been raining, and the missing cows had appeared right next to the road.

His report was met with scepticism and ridicule. In an effort to validate his claims, he underwent hypnotism, during which he recalled that he had passed out when he saw the bright light, and that when he came round, he was in a strange room being examined by small creatures and a tall man with a beard.

This story was met with the same derision by his colleagues, but made international news, and shortly after, Godfrey was called into the inspector's office and confronted by a stranger introducing himself as "the Man from the Ministry". Citing the Official Secrets Act, he made the police constable swear to remain silent about what he had seen.

Was the stranger an MI5 agent guarding top-secret information about alien encounters – or the KGB? Or was he really from the West Yorkshire Police, trying to prevent any further bad publicity at the height of the Yorkshire Ripper case? Had someone staged an attack on Godfrey to resemble accounts of alien abductions?

Perhaps Godfrey wished he had stayed silent. After leaving the police (he claimed to have been hounded out), he said, "I wish I'd never seen the UFO, particularly because of the effects on my children." Years later, he told the *Huddersfield Daily Examiner* that what he saw under hypnosis was likely a dream, but the strange craft he saw was real. What happened to Adamski and those missing minutes will, in all probability, remain a mystery forever.

MANTELL UFO: A STEEP CLIMB TO OBLIVION

Just six months after the discovery at Roswell, on 7 January 1948, a 25-year-old American fighter pilot became not only the first member of the Kentucky Air National Guard to die in flight, but also the first fatality from an encounter with an unidentified flying object.

Several reports had come in of an unusual airborne object – described as "very white", "about one fourth the size of the full moon" and "having the appearance of a flaming red cone trailing a gaseous green mist" – being spotted moving very quickly westwards over Kentucky.

At around 1.45 p.m., officers in the Fort Knox control tower at Godman Army Airfield told four already airborne P-51 Mustang fighter planes from the Kentucky Air National Guard to approach it. One was low on fuel and had to return to base, leaving the other three to set off in steep pursuit, all the while maintaining radio communication with the control tower.

Captain Thomas F. Mantell, a Second World War veteran, was one of the pilots. The air traffic controllers heard him say something indistinct that some interpreted as "metallic and of tremendous size". The other two pilots later reported that although they too had seen an object, it was too small and indistinct to be identifiable. They called off their pursuit at 22,500 feet but Mantell, ignoring the suggestion that they level their altitude to try and see the object more clearly, continued to climb. According to the US Air Force report, once he passed 25,000 feet, he blacked out from lack of oxygen and his plane started to spiral down towards the ground.

He crashed on a farm on the Tennessee border. When his body was pulled from the wreckage, firemen noted that his watch had stopped at 3.18 p.m. – the time of his death. By 3.50 p.m., the object was no longer visible from the Fort Knox control tower.

The incident received significant press coverage, with various unsubstantiated rumours circulating: that it had been a Soviet missile; that Mantell's body had been riddled with bullets from the alien spacecraft that shot him down when he got too close; that his body had been missing from the wreckage; that the plane had completely disintegrated in the air; that the wreckage was radioactive...

As to what the mysterious object had actually been, word went out initially that it had turned out to be the planet Venus. But by 1952, it had been concluded that Venus wasn't bright enough to have been seen by Mantell and the other witnesses that day. The suggestion was then put forward that it might have been a US Navy Skyhook balloon, made of reflective aluminium, large, metallic and secret at the time – also disputed as no such balloon could definitively be said to have been in the area then.

Regardless, US Air Force Captain Edward J. Ruppelt, the man generally credited with coining the term "unidentified flying object" (UFO), described the fatal crash as one of the "classic" UFO cases from 1948 that not only defined the UFO phenomenon in the public mind, but also convinced air force intelligence specialists that UFOs were "real". No longer was talk of flying saucers relegated to the press's "silly season": the fact that someone had died in an alleged alien encounter meant that UFOs, previously thought of as benign and harmless, might actually be hostile and dangerous.

FLATWOODS MONSTER

At 7.15 p.m. on 12 September 1952, it was dusk when schoolboys Edward and Fred May, aged 13 and 12, and their friend Tommy Hyer, allegedly spotted a mysteriously bright object crossing the night sky over the town of Flatwoods, West Virginia, seeming to crash-land on a local farmer's property. Speculating it was a UFO landing, the boys were excited to investigate. They stopped on the way at the Mays' house and continued to the wooded hill with Mrs May and a young National Guardsman, Eugene Lemon, hoping to find out what it was.

On reaching the top of the hill, they claimed to have seen a pulsing red light. Lemon shone his torch in the direction of the light, at which point he said a ten-foot-tall humanoid figure with "a head that resembled the ace of spades", and with greenish-orange glowing eyes and small claw-like hands, levitated off the ground and started gliding towards them. They also smelled a "pungent mist". He dropped the torch and the group turned tail and ran in terror. Later some of the party said they fainted, vomited and had sore throats for several hours.

According to the *Charleston Daily Mail*, several men went to investigate less than an hour later and discovered nothing but a slightly nauseating odour in the air, and possible heat waves.

Mrs May and the guardsman were seen to be clearly shaken by their sighting of the figure, which they claimed had the shape of a man, a red face and green body.

When the local sheriff and deputy searched the area of the alleged encounter with what came to be known as the Flatwoods monster (as well as the Braxton County monster and "Braxie"), they found and smelled nothing. However, the following day, a local newspaper reporter claimed to have found skid marks and an "odd, gummy deposit" in the area. UFO groups subsequently cited this as evidence of an extraterrestrial landing, and alien mania surged through the whole country.

Half a century later, an investigation of the case concluded that the exaggerated nature of the eyewitnesses' account, as well as their subsequent sickness, were probably down to the group's heightened state of anxiety at the time. The bright light in the sky was likely to have been the meteor that was observed across West Virginia that same night. The pulsing red light could possibly have been one of the three aircraft navigation beacons visible from the area of the sighting, whose reflected beams would have accounted for the glowing eyes.

Some say the group's description of the monster that flew towards them closely resembled that of a startled barn owl with its talons gripping a branch, although what they claimed to see was a ten-foot-tall, colourful humanoid figure. Others have pointed out that the reported symptoms of nausea were also very similar to those resulting from exposure to mustard gas... "Those people were the most scared people I've ever seen," said a local newspaperman.

In fact, there had been a report just 5 miles away of a ball of fire that, terrifyingly, transformed into the dark figure of a man. Could someone have rigged up some kind of copycat hoax? If so, they were busy, as just the next day, another local family were allegedly in a country area in the dark when their car broke down and a strange bright light appeared, followed by a ten-foot-tall "reptilian" creature that dragged its claw across their car.

AREA 51: ALIENS UNDER WRAPS?

Although it was first selected as a flight-testing facility for the brand new U-2 reconnaissance aircraft as long ago as 1955, the Area 51 US Air Force-administered complex in Southern Nevada remained under wraps until 2013, when the government finally officially acknowledged its existence.

Area 51 at Groom Lake, a dry lakebed 85 miles north of Las Vegas, covers millions of acres of barren desert land, yet few people know for sure what goes on there today. The official word is that Area 51 is used as a test and training facility – though now for drones rather than reconnaissance aircraft – but it has remained completely inaccessible to the general public, and flying in its airspace is still illegal. What's more, the airbase does not appear on any map, though images from a Russian satellite have shown that an aircraft hangar has been built there in recent years. This secrecy and covert activity has fostered numerous conspiracy theories speculating on the "true" function of Area 51 – theories that mainly involve extraterrestrial activity and are thus linked to Roswell.

The connection between Area 51 and UFOs is not a recent development. The US Central Intelligence Agency (CIA) has had a UFO office specifically to deal with UFO sightings over Nevada since 1950 – probably owing to the spike in such reports when the sinister-looking U-2 spy plane had its first test flights there. It's also possible that the CIA deliberately cultivated the burgeoning UFO mythology in order to cover up what was *actually* going on at Area 51.

In 1989, Robert Lazar added fuel to the fire by claiming that he had worked inside Area 51 and could verify that it was being used by the government to examine UFOs. Not only had he worked on alien technology there, he said, but he had also seen medical photographs of aliens.

Strengthening this link even further, there have been numerous UFO sightings above or close to the military installation, as well as claims by some that they have been abducted by aliens while in the vicinity, and have been experimented on before being returned to Earth.

Still others have speculated that Area 51 may be the manufacturing site of the mysterious and infamous "black helicopters" that are claimed to have pursued vehicles in various locations across the US, as well as to have sprayed a substance that killed animals and vegetation over a wide area. If these helicopters truly exist, whether they have a link to aliens or to the US government, their mission would not seem to be one of peace.

Alternatively, did some aliens survive after their spacecraft crash-landed on Earth, and are they deliberately being kept alive in Area 51? If they are, and if one day, with their far superior technology, they managed to escape, could this spell catastrophe for our planet?

If anyone holds any answers, they're likely to remain tight-lipped on the subject. Until, perhaps, it's too late...

WESTALL FLYING SAUCER

At approximately 11 a.m. on 6 April 1966, a student at Westall High School in Melbourne ran into the school shouting that there was a "flying saucer" outside, and around 200 people including students and a science teacher went outside to take a look.

They subsequently claimed to have seen a grey or silvery-green cigar-shaped flying object about twice as big as a car descending, flying over the school, then landing nearby and disappearing behind trees. Twenty minutes later it took off again, ascending quickly and vanishing out of sight. The teacher, Andrew Greenwood, said that he saw five small aircraft hovering around the object.

In less than an hour, military personnel armed with equipment poured into the area, forming a tight security barrier around the trampled grass circle where the object had landed.

At the time, the alleged sighting was explained away by some as having been nothing more than a weather balloon with a number of small aeroplanes circling around it. However, no commercial, private or military planes had reported anything unusual in the area at that time.

It was decades later that Greenwood, by now retired, claimed that military officers had come round to his house soon after the sighting and told him to remain silent about the incident.

"I was threatened. I was told that I should not say anything about it," he said. "When I tried to explain to them that they weren't there, I was and I knew what I saw, well, the first suggestion was that you'd be ill advised to go on saying that because clearly you were drunk on duty and will have to be reported to the education department and of course you will lose your job."

Greenwood also said that he was interviewed by Dr James E. McDonald, an American physicist known for his interest in UFOs, perhaps on the orders of the US president, Lyndon B. Johnson.

Some have said the object was likely to have been a high-altitude balloon of the type that had been used to monitor radiation levels in the area following the British nuclear tests at Maralinga in South Australia from 1956 to 1963. As for the five circling aircraft, sceptics have suggested that they were simply taking part in an exercise that was known to be used by the Royal Australian Air Force at the time, where one of the planes towed a nylon target windsock-like drogue and the others chased it.

Greenwood always remained convinced, however, that there was something very unusual about what he saw that day in 1966. "I saw a craft. A mechanical object intelligently controlled hovering above me."

ALIENS LOOK FOR WEAPONS AT WOOMERA

A nuclear-weapons-testing facility located in the remote outback of South Australia, more than 250 miles north of Adelaide, became the epicentre of a spate of UFO sightings in the 1950s and 60s, including classic reports of extremely bright lights moving parallel to the ground, and a cigar-shaped craft with a rear exhaust.

In late July of 1960, the weapons-testing facility produced a confidential report describing in great detail the sightings that had taken place in that area on the fifteenth of that month. Dozens of witnesses were interviewed, including two members of the Commonwealth Police and various personnel. One of the police constables attested that he was sitting in his caravan when his attention was drawn to a "light, of approximately the power of bright moonlight, playing on the ground". He left the caravan and saw what he described as a white light travelling from east to west. It turned to a red colour and he thought, at first, that it was a balloon afire and reported it as such. The light appeared to occupy 1½ to 2 degrees of the horizon and the constable thought that the light burned for 30 seconds.

The thoroughness of the investigations and of the wording in this report most likely represented an attempt by the authorities to control unwelcome public interest in the site, where, in addition to the nuclear weapons testing, a space programme was being developed.

Although these sightings occurred during the height of the Cold War (1945–1990), when tension between the Soviet Union and the West was palpable and paranoia raged, some UFO researchers weren't so sure that this was the reason behind the sightings. Instead, they claimed the top-secret nature of the testing would naturally pique the interest of inquisitive extraterrestrial visitors to Earth.

By the 1970s, there were so many UFO sightings in Australia that the Royal Australian Air Force produced pro-forma questionnaires to be given to members of the public who reported having seen a UFO, and provided summaries of such sightings.

FINNISH ENCOUNTER WITH LITTLE GREEN MEN

Early in February 1971, two inexplicable encounters in remote parts of Finland would leave four people haunted for the rest of their days, and others coming up with out-of-this-world answers as to what really happened.

The first, on the evening of 2 February, occurred on an empty stretch of road in the Kiiminki region. From their car, two women spotted a strange light passing over their vehicle and then following them as they continued driving towards the city of Oulu. When the light suddenly vanished, events took a truly bizarre turn, according to both women, who claimed that a short figure in a greenish-brown suit and a helmet then crossed the road in front of them in a series of small jumps.

It was at that point that the terrified driver sped away. Neither woman investigated the matter any further, strangely. But that was not to be the end of the story.

Three days later, 120 miles further south, two young lumberjacks were about to pack up their tools after a morning of felling trees when one of them, 21-year-old Petter Aliranta, noticed a strange metallic object shaped like two saucers hovering just above the trees. He described it as around 15 feet across and with four thin landing legs, each about 6 feet long, with rounded bases.

As he stared at the descending craft, a circular door opened at its base, and as it landed, an odd-looking short creature dressed in a green one-piece suit and a helmet similar to that on an old-fashioned diving suit floated out, landed in the snow, and instead of sinking into it, started to approach the terrified lumberjack, who fired up his chainsaw in response.

The other lumberjack, 18-year-old Esko Juhani Sneck, who had continued working with his chainsaw, had been unaware of the bizarre events unfolding around him until he heard the other chainsaw start up again. He watched, dumbfounded, as the strange green creature suddenly turned back towards the saucer-like craft, with Aliranta bravely giving chase.

Aliranta claimed that as he approached the craft, he could see other vaguely humanoid creatures staring out through three upper windows. As the green creature got close to the craft, it started to float up towards the circular door, at which point Aliranta grabbed hold of its right boot – only to leap back in pain, as the creature's suit was as hot as an iron.

The flying saucer started to buzz and then silently rose up into the atmosphere, disappearing within 15 seconds. Both men claimed to have been unable to talk and scarcely able to move for the next hour. The only evidence that remained, apart from their accounts, consisted of round marks in the snow left, they claimed, by the landing legs. The burn marks on Aliranta's hands apparently remained for several months.

Sceptics say it was a hoax orchestrated by a local radio DJ who persuaded the lumberjacks to go along with it. So many elements of the story are familiar from previous stories of alien encounters. The two women would also have had to be in on the joke. But there are those who still firmly believe that aliens did indeed come on a three-day visit to Finland in the winter of 1971.

BROAD HAVEN TRIANGLE

An area of Wales became such a hotspot for UFO sightings in one particular year that it became known as the Broad Haven Triangle. Multiple witnesses, including a farmer, a hotelier, a local councillor and two groups of schoolchildren, claimed to see an airborne object that most of them described as a typically cigar-shaped spacecraft, with some also seeing tall, slender beings in silver suits close by.

Events took an extraterrestrial turn in Pembrokeshire, south-west Wales, on 4 February 1977, when 14 ten-year-old pupils from Broad Haven Primary School claimed to have seen a UFO landing close to the school playground. The sceptical headmaster separated the children and asked them each to draw what they had seen. Astonishingly, they all drew virtually the same thing – an elongated cigar-shaped spacecraft with a dome at the top.

One of the children, Dave Davies, speaking about the incident more than four decades later, said:

"Throughout the day children had come in from playtime saying they had seen a weird object flying around the perimeter of the school. The headmaster thought he was having his leg pulled at the time so he wouldn't actually go out and have a

look. At the end of the day the final bell went and I thought I'd investigate for myself so I went up to the top perimeter of the school and the object popped up from behind some trees. It was about 50 feet long, about the size of a bus with a fluorescence to it. I felt this uncontrollable urge to run away from what I was seeing. I took one glance behind as I was running away to see it disappearing down behind the trees."

On the same day, before they could have been influenced by any media reports, a group of 20 schoolchildren in Hubberston, 6 miles away, saw what appeared to be a cigar-shaped spacecraft hovering above their school.

Later in 1977, Rosa Granville, the down-to-earth owner of the Haven Fort Hotel near Broad Haven, was woken up by a buzzing noise she initially thought was the gas boiler that she must have forgotten to switch off. But when she reached the kitchen, she realized the noise was coming from outside. Looking out, she saw an oval object with lights that was slowly landing. Two figures she referred to as "creatures" in silver suits were emerging. They had very long arms and legs, their heads covered in helmets.

Rosa's daughter Francine, speaking in 2016 about the incident, said the craft left a small crater in the ground that remained there decades later. In a letter her mother wrote to her local Member of Parliament, she said the incident had left her feeling "agitated and disturbed and not the least bit desirous of another encounter". In the same area that year, a farmer and his wife were surprised late one evening by a tall silver-suited being staring at them through the window. They contacted the police, who found that an intense heat source in the garden had scorched a rosebush.

To this day, none of the Broad Haven children – who have remained forever linked to that memorable day in 1977 – have changed their story or said they were lying. Sceptics put the sightings down to mistakenly identified military aircraft, sewage lorries or farm machinery – or just to children's make-believe or adult hoaxes. But if hoaxes, they were certainly elaborate. Early one morning in the same year, local councillor Cyril John saw a grey egg-shaped object with a bright orange-red light on top and a tall silver-suited humanoid figure, both hovering in the air for 25 minutes before drifting away.

FREDERICK VALENTICH: TAKEN OVER TASMANIA

On the evening of 21 October 1978, 20-year-old Australian pilot Frederick Valentich was flying a Cessna light aircraft over the Bass Strait separating mainland Australia from Tasmania, bound for King Island. He had told flight officials that he was picking up some friends there, while he told others he was going for crayfish, both of which were later found to be false. He had also failed to inform the island's airport of his intention to land there.

During the flight, he reported that an aircraft, appearing to toy with him, had passed at high speed just over 300 yards above him. He described it as having a shiny metal surface and a green light. When asked to identify it, he then replied, "It's not an aircraft." The transmission was interrupted by metallic scraping noises for 17 seconds before all contact was lost.

A four-day sea and air search covering 1,000 square miles was mounted to find the missing pilot but ceased on 25 October with no result. An investigation into Valentich's disappearance could find no cause, but it was consequently presumed that the incident had been fatal.

Valentich was described by his father as a firm believer in UFOs, who had been worried about being attacked by them. UFO investigators seized on the disappearance and on reports at that time of a green light moving erratically in the sky, taking it all as evidence that extraterrestrials had either destroyed Valentich's aircraft or abducted him. They backed up their claims with photos taken by a plumber on the day of the disappearance, showing – albeit not very clearly – an "unknown flying object, of moderate dimensions", exiting the water at speed and "apparently surrounded by a cloud-like vapour/exhaust residue".

Others, not convinced, suggested that Valentich had staged his own disappearance, and that he might not even have been flying where he claimed to be, as at no point was his aircraft plotted on radar. Melbourne police, on the other hand, reported a light aircraft making a mysterious landing near Cape Otway – close to where Valentich had claimed to be – at the same time as he disappeared.

Alternatively, some have proposed that the inexperienced young pilot – although a member of the Royal Australian Air Force Training Corps, he had been rejected for the Royal Australian Air Force (RAAF), failed so far to receive his commercial pilot's licence and been noted in other unorthodox incidents – had become disorientated and was unknowingly flying upside down, so that the lights he claimed to see had in fact been his own, reflected in the water, which he then crashed into. Although his Cessna aircraft could not have flown upside down for long, five years later, an engine cowl flap washed up on Flinders Island, north-east of Tasmania, and was identified as having come from the same type of aircraft Valentich had been flying.

While suicide was virtually eliminated as a possibility by Valentich's doctors and colleagues, experts who reviewed the radio transcripts and other data thought he might have been trying to compensate for what he wrongly took to be a tilted horizon, putting the aircraft into a downward "graveyard spiral", and mistaking the planets Venus, Mars and Mercury and the bright star Antares for the overhead stationary lights that he had reported seeing.

The mystery of what happened to Frederick Valentich is one that only he knows the answer to, wherever he ended up. Whether it was a watery grave or, as his father continued to believe, captive on some distant planet, we will likely never know.

JAPAN AIRLINES CARGO FLIGHT 1628 (BEAUJOLAIS UFO)

On 17 November 1986, a Japanese cargo aircraft was involved in a UFO incident that resulted in the experienced captain being grounded for several years afterwards.

Japan Airlines Flight 1628 was en route from Paris to Narita International Airport near Tokyo with a cargo of Beaujolais wine. Over eastern Alaska, just after sunset, the crew spotted two unidentified objects to their left, which they initially assumed were military aircraft, but which then rose abruptly from below and closed in to escort their aircraft. Captain Kenju Terauchi radioed Anchorage to ask about other aircraft in the area; the control tower was not aware of other traffic but was picking up other craft intermittently.

As the strange aircraft got closer, Captain Terauchi felt the heat on his face of what appeared to be grids of engine thrusters glowing so brightly that they lit up the cargo plane's cockpit. Then the two objects departed, but a third disc-shaped object that Terauchi referred to as the "mothership", being "twice the size of an aircraft carrier", started following them.

The incident lasted for 50 minutes, ending over the high mountain peak of Denali. No other aircraft in the vicinity had been able to make out the UFOs, though Terauchi later described the objects in detail, using both words and drawings to show how the objects had seemed to fly "as if there was no such thing as gravity".

Following the incident, Terauchi stated in the official Federal Aviation Administration (FAA) report that the objects had been UFOs, and in December 1986 he gave an interview to two Japanese TV journalists. As a result of talking to the press, he was grounded by Japanese Airlines and moved to a desk job, only being reinstated as a pilot several years later.

John Callahan, the FAA division chief of the Accidents and Investigations branch, speculated that what the crew had seen was an early flight of a stealth bomber, which was in the process of being developed. When he and his boss played a video of the radar data and voice tapes to the then-administrator of the FAA, Donald D. Engen, Engen asked them not to talk to anyone about it until given approval, and to prepare a presentation of the data for a group of government officials, including representatives of the FBI, the CIA and President Ronald Reagan's Scientific Study Team. After the presentation the next day, everyone present was told that the incident was secret and that their meeting "never took place". According to Callahan, the government officials considered the information they had just seen on the video the first instance of recorded radar data on a UFO, and they took possession of it (though he managed to retain the original video and documents).

Some UFO researchers viewed the incident with scepticism, with paranormal investigator Robert Sheaffer writing, "The bottom line is, Terauchi's own flight crew saw only 'lights', and other aircraft checking out the situation saw nothing unusual." Nevertheless, the sighting attracted widespread media coverage as a rare instance of UFOs apparently having been tracked on both ground and airborne radar, while also being observed by an experienced team of airline pilots and subsequently confirmed by an FAA division chief.

In 1987, the FAA stated that the unusual data were due to a "split radar image". In a 1997 book, UFO researcher Philip J. Klass said the FAA called Terauchi a "UFO repeater", having previously made claims of UFO sightings, though all three crew members gave evidence.

Whether or not the cargo remained intact was not mentioned by anyone involved in the investigation into the crew's apparent extraterrestrial sighting.

RENDLESHAM FOREST INCIDENT: "BRITAIN'S ROSWELL"

On a night in late December 1980, in the English county of Suffolk, near Rendlesham Forest and close to RAF Woodbridge, then a US Air Force airbase, military personnel including the deputy base commander, Lieutenant Colonel Charles Halt, and Sergeant Jim Penniston were among those claiming to have seen lights descending into the forest.

In January 1981, Halt wrote a detailed memo to the UK Ministry of Defence entitled "Unexplained Lights". In it, he described what he claimed to have seen, stating that they initially thought they had witnessed a crashing aircraft. When they went to investigate, however, they came across a glowing metallic object with coloured lights. As they approached the object, it started to move through the trees, at which point, Halt claimed, "the animals on a nearby farm went into a frenzy".

When the servicemen returned to the site in the light of day, they found a clearing with three small impressions arranged in a triangle, as well as burn marks and trees with broken branches. Two days later, they undertook a further investigation to detect radiation levels in the area. As well as recording higher levels of radiation in the clearing, they also reported seeing a flashing light to the east.

They could at the same time see the light from the Orfordness Lighthouse. As one of the UK's brightest lighthouses at the time, some have said this must have been the actual source of light claimed to have been from UFOs, though here it clearly wasn't. Later during the same investigation, the servicemen saw three star-like lights in the sky, the brightest hovering for two or three hours and appearing occasionally to beam down a stream of light. Astronomers have explained these as simply bright stars.

In a 2003 television documentary, Penniston revealed a notebook purporting to give many more details of what he observed on the night, including pictorial symbols on the strange craft and the fact that it took off at an "impossible" speed. He claimed they were told that what they had seen was top secret and the photos they had taken were overexposed.

In June 2010, Halt signed an affidavit stating that he believed the sightings to truly have been of extraterrestrials, and that both the UK and US authorities had deliberately covered the incident up. Sceptics have pointed to contradictions between the affidavit and his earlier memo. In the same year as the affidavit was signed, Colonel Theodore "Ted" Conrad, the base commander of Woodbridge in 1980, provided his own statement about the incident: "We saw nothing that resembled Lieutenant Colonel Halt's descriptions either in the sky or on the ground... We had people in position to validate Halt's narrative, but none of them could."

However, a 1983 article in the now-defunct science-fiction magazine *Omni* claimed that Conrad "began a brief investigation of the incident... [He] did interview two of the eyewitnesses and concludes, 'Those lads saw something, but I don't know what it was.'"

The lights may, according to some doubters, have come from a farmhouse or Orfordness lighthouse, or from a meteor; and the three impressions in the clearing might have been made by an animal. No concrete evidence for a landing in the forest ever emerged, and UFO researcher David Clarke concluded that the story was a hoax. Or, as put more gently by reporter Jenny Randles, perhaps it was simply "a series of misperceptions of everyday things encountered in less than everyday circumstances".

Whatever the reality, however, the UK Forestry Commission has commemorated the sightings with a monument and a "UFO Trail". Not everyone, it seems, is a sceptic.

ARIEL SCHOOL CLOSE ENCOUNTER AT PLAYTIME

In September 1994, a wave of UFO mania was sweeping across Zimbabwe, sparked by numerous reports of a bright fireball travelling at speed through the night sky. Although some thought it was a comet or meteor – or even a disintegrating rocket booster from a Russian satellite – others were convinced they had just had a close encounter with aliens. Adding further to an already charged climate were UFO claims by a young boy and his mother, and by a trucker who said he had come across alien beings on a road.

Then on 14 September, during a 15-minute unsupervised break at Ariel School – a private school in Ruwa, a small area not far from Harare – 62 children ran back inside screaming, saying they had seen silver aircraft and aliens descending from the sky. Initially, their teachers put the alleged mass sighting down to nothing more than a practical joke. But after hearing the strange accounts, parents came in the next day demanding to know what had happened. The children were asked to draw pictures of what they had seen, and the pictures were the same.

By no means did all the children at Ariel School claim to have seen anything strange that day. But those who claimed they did, children aged between eight and twelve, together with their teachers and the BBC reporter who first covered the story, were interviewed by John E. Mack, head of the psychiatry department at Harvard Medical School in the US, who visited the school. Mack had a particular interest in UFOs and the alien abduction phenomenon. In the interviews, many of the children's accounts contained similar details.

They all described one or more silver objects, usually discs, appearing in the sky and then floating down onto a field just beyond the school property. Between one and four creatures with big eyes and dressed completely in black came out of some sort of aircraft and approached the children, many of whom cried in fear then ran, though some – mostly the older pupils – carried on watching as the aliens came nearer.

What's surprising about the episode is that the unidentified visitors communicated an environmental message to the children by telepathy. The younger children, who wouldn't have known about telepathy, still clearly recounted the message:

Child: What I thought was maybe the world is going to end maybe they telling us the world's gonna end.

Mack: Well why do you think they might want us to be scared?

Child: Because maybe because we don't look after the planet and the air.

Mack: Is this an idea that you have had before that we don't look after the planet properly or the air or did this idea come to you when you had this experience?

Child: When I had this experience.

An 11-year-old girl said, "I think they want people to know that we're actually making harm on this world and we mustn't get too technologed."

Would the concepts of telepathy and human beings' responsibility for the well-being of the planet have been new to most of the children? The jury's out on that. The school was an expensive, mostly white establishment and the children would have had access to television. But several of the eyewitnesses have continued to maintain that their accounts were true. The event rapidly became one of Africa's most famous UFO cases – and perhaps helped spread the word about a need for respecting our own planet.

THE "TIC TAC"

"It's white. It has no wings. It has no rotors. I go, 'Holy sh*t, what is that?'" said Commander David Fravor, whose elite Black Aces squadron had been taking part in training exercises over the Pacific Ocean on the afternoon of 14 November 2004 before being diverted to new coordinates for a "real-world intercept".

An encounter with a mysterious airborne object zigzagging at high speed off the coast of Southern California left the highly trained US Navy fighter pilot so puzzled by what he had seen that he could only describe it as resembling a giant Tic Tac mint.

"This thing would go from one way to another, similar to if you threw a ping-pong ball against the wall," he explained.

The pilot acting as wingman that day, Alex Dietrich, now a retired lieutenant commander, recalled noticing that the ocean was churning in a strange way immediately before the odd-looking craft came into view. As they attempted to intercept it, she said, "It was so unpredictable – high G, rapid velocity, rapid acceleration. So you're wondering: How can I possibly fight this?"

But, according to Commander Fravor, in a split second, the object turned, rapidly accelerated, flew across the nose of his fighter jet, and disappeared.

The object was just one of hundreds of similar "anomalous aerial vehicles" (or AAVs – the US Navy's term for UFOs) that the missile cruiser USS *Princeton* had been picking up on its radar system over the previous few days. One pilot managed to get video footage of the "Tic Tac" craft, using an infrared camera. As it disappeared into the distance, others appeared, and more jets were instructed to take off from the USS *Nimitz* carrier to try to intercept them.

The incident wasn't known about publicly until 2017, when *The New York Times* published an article about it and also released the fighter pilot's video footage. In 2019, the US Navy announced that it was drafting new guidelines for the reporting of such objects to make it easier for military personnel to talk about AAV sightings without fear of ridicule.

But even if the Navy takes such matters seriously, the "Tic Tac" incident also attracted many sceptics, some claiming that it and the other mysterious objects seen at that time were merely advanced reconnaissance drones.

Whoever is right – the highly trained naval personnel who had never seen anything like the objects they witnessed, or the doubters – one thing is fairly certain: they weren't gigantic fresh-breath mints.

DON'T EAT YOUR GREENS OR YOU'LL END UP AN ALIEN

The village of Woolpit in Suffolk, England, bears the silhouettes of two children on its sign. Their story was originally recounted by Ralph of Coggeshall and William of Newburgh, writers in the twelfth and early thirteenth centuries, and although their accounts vary slightly in their details, they tell an unusual tale. Sometime in the twelfth century, two young children with green skin and odd-looking clothes are said to have suddenly appeared in Woolpit. They spoke in a strange language and wouldn't eat anything the villagers offered them, until they came across some raw broad beans, which they consumed greedily.

The villagers took the children in, and they gradually started eating other food and eventually lost their green hue. At around the time they were to be baptized, the boy became ill and died. According to Ralph, the girl was considered "very wanton and impudent", but she adjusted to life in the village and learned to speak English. She was then able to explain that she and her brother had come from a place that she called Saint Martin's Land, where it was always twilight because there was no sunshine, and everything was green. The villagers

301

called the girl Agnes, and she went on to marry a royal official named Richard Barre.

Although William referred to the story as "strange and prodigious", neither he nor Ralph offered any explanation. But their reticence hasn't stopped others down the centuries from seeking answers to the mystery of the green homeless children.

In 1621, Robert Burton suggested simply that the children "fell from Heaven". In a 1996 article, the astronomer Duncan Lunan laid out a rather more complex extraterrestrial scenario, proposing that the children had been accidentally transported from their home planet due to a "matter transmitter" malfunction, and that their green skin was the result of their consumption back home of genetically modified alien plants.

Other more earthbound explanations have included the possibility that the children were drugged and kidnapped, or were the orphans of Flemish mercenaries who ended up wandering, disorientated, into Woolpit in their strange Flemish clothes, suffering from a dietary deficiency that left them with a greenish pallor.

Whichever explanation is closest to the truth, the green children of Woolpit have been the inspiration behind countless works of art, from stories and poems to plays and operas – and even the name of an Anglo-Norwegian pop duo. It's certainly the earliest account of little green people, and perhaps a good example of how to welcome friendly aliens.

FINAL WORD

This wide-ranging look at unsolved mysteries has visited many parts of the world and has swept from prehistory right up to the present day.

Some of the unsolvable cases presented are undeniably tragic; the loved ones of people who went missing – never to be seen or heard from again – would spend the rest of their lives tormented, wondering what happened but never knowing for sure, and never willing or able to give up the hope that one day that person would just walk in through the door.

Other mysteries – such as inexplicable sightings of ghostly apparitions, demonic wild cats on remote moorland, silver-suited men disembarking from dome-shaped spacecraft or the awe-inspiring sight of a seemingly impossible prehistoric megalith – may leave a tingle thrilling down the spine.

When it comes down to it, it's undeniable that we all love a good mystery. The very fact of not knowing exactly what happened is what makes it all so utterly compelling and an endless source of fascination, while also being frustratingly impenetrable. Once you've turned the last page of this book, be prepared for your mind to revisit the people, places and things that have graced the pages, never quite letting you close the door on all the unanswered questions that endure to this day.